SEMISWEET

SEMISWEET

An Orphan's Journey Through the School the Hersheys Built

John A. O'Brien

ROWMAN & LITTLEFIELD
Lanham • Boulder • New York • Toronto • Plymouth, UK

Published by Rowman & Littlefield
4501 Forbes Boulevard, Suite 200, Lanham, Maryland 20706
www.rowman.com

10 Thornbury Road, Plymouth PL6 7PP, United Kingdom

British Library Cataloguing in Publication Information Available

Library of Congress Cataloging-in-Publication Data

O'Brien, John A., 1943–
Semisweet : an orphan's journey through the school the Hersheys built / John A. O'Brien.
pages cm
Includes bibliographical references.
ISBN 978-1-4422-3257-0 (cloth : alk. paper) — ISBN 978-1-4422-3258-7 (electronic : alk. paper)
Milton Hershey School (Hershey, Pa.)—History. 2. Orphans—Education—Pennsylvania—Hershey—History. 3. Poor children—Education—Pennsylvania—Hershey—History. 4. O'Brien, John A., 1943– I. Title.
LD7501.H47O27 2014
371.0086'945—dc23
2014006846

∞™ The paper used in this publication meets the minimum requirements of American National Standard for Information Sciences Permanence of Paper for Printed Library Materials, ANSI/NISO Z39.48-1992.

Printed in the United States of America

To Frankie who deserved a little love in his lifetime
and
To Milton and Catherine Hershey whose generosity was
even sweeter than his chocolate.

There is a destiny that makes us brothers
None goes his way alone
All that we send into the lives of others
Comes back into our own.

—Edwin Markham, poet (1852–1940)

A tribute to HomeGuys and HomeGals everywhere

CONTENTS

PREFACE

I wrote *Semisweet* to tell you and the whole world about the most remarkable school on earth: the Milton Hershey School. But what makes this "orphanage" remarkable is not that it has a trust exceeding $10 billion and owns controlling interest of the Hershey Company—a Fortune 500 corporation. That is extraordinary too. But I wrote this saga to trumpet the school's founders' unparalleled generosity and on-going mission to serve and save thousands of the neediest children in America—from 1909, and "in perpetuity" no less. Thanks to Milton and Catherine Hershey, the Milton Hershey School is one of the rare places on the planet where inordinate resources and a sacred mission combine to produce a miracle.

I wrote *Semisweet* as a forthright account of the school based upon my sixty-two-year journey through it, first as an orphan toddler, through my teens and then as an alumni protest leader, and finally as president of Milton Hershey School. In stunning full-circle fashion, I was asked to help save the school that had saved my life. My fellow time-traveler through the rough and tumble orphanage of the 1950s is my older brother, Frankie. He would not be so lucky.

Because I am the narrator of the *Semisweet* journey, this account is partly my memoir. Since it would be impossible to remember all the details of the events of my childhood or the precise words of actual conversations, I have selected memorable highlights and attempted to recreate the feeling, tone, and essence of those events. My intent was to chronicle my experience and perceptions accurately while minimizing harm to anyone.

In that spirit, I use fictional names for characters portrayed in a critical light when it would be neither useful nor necessary to discern their identities. For example, anyone depicted as a bully is given a fictional name. And the houseparents called "the Weavers" are composite characters based upon several houseparent couples I had during my years at different farmhomes. The "good guys"—like my mentors the Arbogasts, the Bikles, Bill Fisher, and Coach Klingler; and my buddies like Carmen and Percy—all have their real names.

Millions of people know firsthand about delicious Hershey Chocolate. But relatively few people know about the remarkable school Mr. Hershey's chocolate built. Hopefully, *Semisweet* will expose you to the life-saving deeds—and the challenges—of this little-known national treasure. And as you contemplate Milton Hershey School's inexhaustible treasure, you may want to think about how this miraculous institution could save even more disadvantaged children. The best is yet to come.

ACKNOWLEDGMENTS

I first want to thank Christine Black, my collaborator, who helped me with the herculean task of reducing my original eight-hundred-page "mammoth-script" to a digestible size. Chris, a former reporter for the *Boston Globe* and CNN, helped me say more in fewer words and make tough choices about what had to be left out to make *Semisweet* a better book. Thanks, Chris, for your inspiration and deft use of a scalpel even when a hatchet was required.

And to my touchstones, Peter Carry, Charlie Gibson, Bert Kerstetter, and Dan White, thank you for your unvarnished feedback. Your truth about focus, feeling, style, and authenticity helped me write smarter and hopefully made this a better read.

A big "hats off" to my HomeGuy readers Carmen Gilotte, Tom McClay, and Nick Nissley who ensured that I captured the unique camaraderie and loneliness of our institutionalized world. And a special thanks to another HomeGuy, Bill Fisher, former Milton Hershey School president, who verified that I got his challenging tenure properly chronicled. For further historical accuracy, I am indebted to Jim McMahon, director of MHS School History, for validating dates, events, and key facts.

In the production department, I appreciate the typing of thousands of draft pages by Tara Leeson, Mary Harding, and Jan Moylan.

Most importantly, bravo to my bride, Gail, for being mostly patient during the emotional cyclone of my dramatic Milton Hershey decade.

Imploring me to "get the damn book finished" was actually very helpful, dear.

The net proceeds from the sale of *Semisweet* will go to a foundation that serves kids like my brother Frankie.

1

MARCHING HOME

Milton Hershey with his first children, 1913. *Courtesy of the Milton Hershey School*

Even in the dim illumination of a slim crescent moon, the contours of the deathly quiet cemetery felt as reassuring as a rare childhood hug. I had been here before and would come again. Although tomorrow promised to be daunting, something compelled me to pay a late-night call to the gravesite of the man and woman who had saved my life. When I was three years old, my brother Frankie and I had been dropped off at Hershey Industrial School in Hershey, Pennsylvania, like bags of soiled laundry—dropped in the hands of those interred here.

Milton Hershey, the chocolate magnate, founded the school for orphaned white boys in 1909. He always said it was "Kitty's idea," referring to his wife, Catherine. But the residential school for destitute boys was clearly a joint venture. The Hersheys were unable to have children of their own, so they effectively adopted thousands of needy children and provided them with a safe haven in the countryside and a chance at a better life. I never met either Milton or Catherine Hershey. They died before my arrival at the school in 1947. But like the old spiritual, I was lost and then found. Frankie would not be so lucky.

The following day, more than fifty years after I first showed up in Hershey as a terrified orphan, I would be inaugurated as the eighth president of the institution now known as the Milton Hershey School. I had been hired to save my school and restore the mission of its founders after more than a decade of turmoil. The night before I was to be installed as president, there was one crucial visit I had to make. My wife Gail had joked that it was like a coronation. But this job had little in common with the duties of a king. She understood that my mind was whirring with anticipation, and I needed time alone.

I headed straight for the gravesite of Milton and Catherine Hershey. The Hershey family gravesite dominates the main entrance of Hershey Cemetery with an impressive marble headstone that reaches about fifteen feet to the heavens and curves like a maternal arm around part of the burial site. It is not ornate. The Hersheys were not ostentatious people.

At this hour, I drove directly to the gravesite. Not too many people visit graveyards after dark. Milton's parents rest beneath the slabs on the right so I favored the left side where Milton was buried next to his beloved Kitty, the lively daughter of Irish immigrants, who died thirty years before he did. My quest was spiritual, not religious. I did not really believe these surrogate parents could hear me. But entering this sacred circle, I felt a mystical connection to the couple who had provided me with a home, an education, and the values that formed me as an adult.

I did not intend to speak out loud, yet I found myself whispering: "Mr. and Mrs. Hershey, I am deeply honored for the privilege of serving your remarkable Home and kids. We need your help, your spirit, more than ever. I pledge to do all that I can to pay back your life-saving gift to me. Your generosity, your vision, will guide us every day. Amen."

The "Amen" did not feel right, but it slipped out, a prayerful punctuation to a heartfelt sentiment. I suddenly felt calmer, more relaxed, and even more certain of my commitment to the challenge I faced the next day. There were no hooting owls or lightning flashes to indicate that someone in another realm heard my prayer, but I somehow sensed the school's founders had my back.

Not quite done, I walked past the car to the special gravesite for students who died while living at the school. The first boy to die, Charles Swartz, lost his life in the influenza epidemic in 1918, just a week before Christmas. Mr. Hershey considered the boys at the school members of his family, "his boys," and he wanted those who died young to be buried near him. The bones of other "HomeGuys" rest near Charles. I prayed this time for the souls of my departed brothers and pledged an all-out effort to restore our Home to the honorable path trod so lightly by these lads.

Years earlier, soon after my arrival in Hershey as a boy, I discovered that the founder of our school had humble beginnings too. Milton Snavely Hershey was born on September 13, 1857, to Fanny Snavely and Henry Hershey in Derry Church, Pennsylvania. His formal education ended by the time he was twelve, but like so many self-made businessmen, he persisted, experimented, and innovated until he realized his dreams. There were many setbacks on the road to success. His father arranged for him to be a printer's apprentice but young Milton hated it and got himself fired after letting his hat fall into the press. He discovered his calling was confections, the creation of candy. His first business ventures went bust despite valiant efforts. Yet he never gave up. He finally created a successful caramel company and then sold it in order to pursue his ultimate dream of producing affordable milk chocolate. His five-cent Hershey chocolate bar and his Hershey Kisses brought real chocolate to the American masses and made him a millionaire many times over.

Greatness is often a matter of luck as well as pluck, and Milton Hershey was lucky to live at an exciting time of growth and opportunity. As he came of age, the United States was moving from the agricultural to the industrial age. After the Civil War, the United States embarked upon an unprecedented period of economic growth. The first flying machine took to the sky, and Bell's telephone and Edison's light bulb burst onto the scene. It was a heady time when a young ambitious man could not be faulted for believing that his achievement was limited only by his imagination. The combustion engine and technological innovation created a plutocracy of exceptionally wealthy men. Milton Hershey was one of them. He and others from his time created enduring American brands like Coca-Cola, Wrigley Chewing Gum, Pillsbury flour, and Lipton tea. The often ruthless and driven entrepreneurs of the era built stunning fortunes from railroads, mines, and manufacturing plants that churned out consumer goods in response to rising demand from a growing middle class.

The era was also marked by exploitation of the working poor, by political corruption, and by a wide and varied range of ethical abuses. In the yin and yang of history, one series of actions triggers a reaction, and the reaction to the worst excesses of industrialization was the Progressive Era and the growth of the American Labor Movement.

M. S. Hershey was one of the good guys. He was not spared labor union troubles in Hershey, and he was not a man without faults, but unlike some of his fellow millionaires, he took a more enlightened view of his workers and a more compassionate view of the needy. Biographers have described him as a mix of the sober Mennonite values of his mother Fanny and the adventure-loving, fortune-hunting instincts of his frequently absent father Henry. He brought the frugal, modest ways of the Pennsylvania Dutch, the so-called plain people, to his chocolate factory and school. And while Milton was grounded in his mother's virtues of hard work and discipline, he was a vivid dreamer like his dad.

At the turn of the twentieth century, Milton Hershey sold his caramel company in Lancaster to a competitor for $1 million, a stunning amount of money at the time. Although he did not yet know how to create an American version of the delicious Swiss chocolate he enjoyed in Europe, he used that money to build his own chocolate factory just thirty miles away. It says a lot about his self-confidence that he built the world's largest chocolate factory in the cornfields of a deserted valley before he had the recipe for his new candy.

To realize his dream of producing milk chocolate, he returned to his birthplace in Dauphin County. He bought up thousands of acres of land, hired a surveyor, and plotted the lines of a community. He had a utopian vision of a humming factory that would produce the first affordable milk chocolate in America, a factory surrounded by a bucolic town with a trolley to carry workers back and forth to work. His plan included all the amenities of an ideal community: parks, flowers and trees, free schools, and a department store. Over time, he funded a hospital, museum, town community center, and dozens of other features that enhanced the quality of life for Hershey residents. During the Great Depression, M. S. Hershey used his money to launch a building spree in Hershey that created jobs and protected Hershey from the economic dislocation suffered by the rest of the country. He truly cared about people. There is a legendary story of how a factory foreman called him to come to the Hotel Hershey construction site in the 1930s and exclaimed, "Mr. Hershey, behold this fantastic invention called the steam shovel. It can do the work of forty men!" Milton Hershey reportedly replied, "Well, get rid of that darn thing and bring back those forty men!"

He was not without complexity. His ingrained frugality and good business sense sometimes competed with his innate kindness. In one annual report, he called for the reduction of bonuses for the ladies (mostly Hershey Kiss inspectors) who had worn a rut in the factory lawn by taking a shortcut to the parking lot. And he reduced the pay for drivers who were allowing their engines to idle during shipment pickups on cold days. But such pettiness was rare. His overall approach made Mr. Hershey more than a benefactor. He was a savior.

To this day Hershey, Pennsylvania, looks like something out of a Norman Rockwell painting, a sweet frozen treat of old-fashioned small-town Americana. The street lights are in the shape of Hershey chocolate kisses, the main streets of the town are called Chocolate Avenue and Cocoa Avenue, and the original two-story homes are still as pristine as the day they were built, reflecting the pride of generations of home owners.

Many of the titans of industry from that time, men such as John D. Rockefeller, Andrew Carnegie, Andrew Mellon, and Cornelius Vanderbilt, became as well known for their philanthropy as they were for their business success. Many of these men are more famous today than Milton Hershey. But in Dauphin County, no one mattered more. I heard his name almost daily throughout my childhood. He was a presence in my life; the benevolent patron who became more powerful than myth to me and my fellow HomeGuys. More than sixty-five years after his death, townspeople and alumni from the school invoke his name and views with a level of familiarity and intimacy that reflects his outsized role in their lives.

Milton Hershey differed from many of the other wealthy philanthropists of his time in another key respect: he was not a death-bed philanthropist who gave away his fortune near the end of his life; he did it while he was still very much alive. He bequeathed most of his fortune, the bulk of stock in his iconic chocolate company, to his boys in the form of a trust in 1918, three years after his beloved wife died and twenty-seven years before his own death. The gift was extraordinary in its generosity at the time: $60 million in 1918, which is the equivalent of more than $900 million today. He did it without notice or fanfare. Few outside his closest circle were aware of it. It was so unusual that the *New York Times* published a major story on the gift a full five years after the fact when word finally leaked out.

He left an extraordinary legacy: the chocolate candy company that still carries his name; the community of Hershey, created whole cloth out of pasture land in Dauphin County; and a unique residential school designed to give the neediest children security, a vocation, and a promising life. With his handpicked trustees, he guided Hershey Industrial School personally until his death. When we alumni rose up in protest years later, we looked back at his track record to find a roadmap of his philosophy and intent.

I grew up at Hershey Industrial School (renamed Milton Hershey School in 1951). I remember nothing of my infancy or toddler years before my arrival. Hershey was Home. The school was my Family. Like all children, I responded at the time with a mixture of gratitude and resentment. Kids usually resent authority, and I was no exception. But as I grew older, my affection for the school grew with my understanding of how the institution changed the course of my life.

As "orphans" we were the objects of sympathy, even pity. But we also felt somewhat ashamed. There is a stigma to institutionalization, even at a school as vaunted as Milton Hershey School. Children who are sent to institutions, whatever the reason, often feel they are given away because they are worthless or "bad." When we went into the town of Hershey for our rare nights out, we swaggered around town in a manner copied from the popular movies of the day—like James Dean or Sal Mineo . . . but our identical institutional shoes gave us away as HomeGuys. Our response to that stigma was to develop a fierce pride in our school. This almost tribal reaction will be familiar to anyone who is "different" from the mainstream. There is something in the human spirit that triggers solidarity in response to group oppression.

I do not dwell on *might have beens* because my life experience has made me a pragmatic man. And I do not question for a second the debt I owe Mr. Hershey and his school. The school gave me the opportunity to get a first-class education at two world-class universities, to raise my own family, and to enjoy success in business. It gave me my life.

That is not to say my experiences were all positive. I lived at the school at a time when some houseparents knew more about raising cows than children; when an angry house father or teacher could whip a boy with impunity; and when a disturbed, angry teenager could abuse a younger, more vulnerable boy while many looked the other way. The school toughened me up and taught me how to survive. But when I compare the good and the bad, I am left with the enduring belief that Milton Hershey School gave me opportunities I would not otherwise have had and made me a man with solid values. It would now be my responsibility to see those values transmitted to the students of the twenty-first century.

The orphan is a time-honored metaphor in literature. From Romulus and Remus, the fabled twin orphan boys raised by wild dogs who founded Rome, and Tom Sawyer, the plucky orphan raised by his Aunt Polly, to Harry Potter, the remarkable young wizard who comes of age at Hogwarts, the orphan has long been a symbol of loss, abandonment, and overcoming great odds. When Hershey Industrial School was created in 1909, there was no government social safety net. Those in distress depended upon the charity of churches, neighbors, and extended family. This makeshift safety net rested upon goodwill.

By the time I arrived at Hershey Industrial School, the Social Security system created in 1935 as part of Franklin D. Roosevelt's New Deal response to the Great Depression was more than ten years old and on its way to providing a level of economic security for the old, the disabled, the widowed, and the orphaned. Government checks began to minimize the need for orphanages and poor houses. Moreover, the mainstream view of orphans and orphanages was changing. Putting fatherless children into an institution was no longer an acceptable option in some quarters. The image of Oliver Twist begging for more gruel in the famous Charles Dickens's tale was sadly reflective of the poor conditions and low standard of care at many of the nearly one thousand orphanages in the United States at the turn of the twentieth century.

The good places, such as Father Flanagan's Boys Town in Nebraska, immortalized by the 1938 movie starring Spencer Tracy, and Hershey Industrial School, were the exceptions. Child-rearing experts recommended keeping children whose parents were unable or unfit to raise them with their extended families or benevolent families in their home communities. The foster system evolved, and government began to provide subsidies to individual families. A modern welfare system replaced the ad hoc support of religious and charitable organizations. Hundreds of orphanages closed in the United States.

The world was changing after World War II when Frankie and I were little boys. But Hershey existed in its own little bubble. At first, it was protected by its founder and patron. Later, his money and the success of his chocolate company reinforced a kind of vapor lock insulating the little town and its school from the changes taking place in the outside world. By the time I returned at the dawn of a new century, the school had been whipsawed by a dozen years of changes. Some of them were well intended and long overdue. But many of us alumni were convinced that some reforms went too far and were destroying the very soul of Milton Hershey School.

The deed of trust drafted under Mr. Hershey's watchful eye created the school in 1909. It is the Magna Carta of Milton Hershey School. It is far more than a legal document, although the legalities would prove to be important and decisive at the end of the twentieth century when we alumni challenged the all-powerful board of managers over the direction of the school. To us, Mr. Hershey left a sacred trust. He was gone, but we HomeGuys felt we knew what he wanted and were impelled by an obligation to carry out his intent to make sure the school continued to serve the neediest children who had the fewest responsible adults in their lives.

Each generation of poor neglected kids deserved a chance to realize their full potential just as we had. We all understood the need to amend the deed of trust to reflect changing times. Mr. Hershey did so several times himself. Some child-rearing practices that were acceptable in 1909 had long fallen out of favor with educators and social scientists. We viewed the deed of trust as a living document based upon a bedrock of immutable fundamental values, much like the U.S. Constitution, which has been amended twenty-seven times but still guides the U.S. Supreme Court in its decisions.

As an active member of the Milton Hershey School Alumni Association, I was deeply involved in the decade of turmoil of the 1990s. I had been hired as a consultant to conduct leadership seminars for the staff in the late 1980s by President William Fisher, who had been my German teacher in high school. President Fisher was a longtime staff member and 1950 graduate who had been named Alumnus of the Year. Then I too was named Alumnus of the Year in 1990, a singular honor for a HomeGuy that only reinforced my intense feelings for the school. As a leader in the alumni protest, I worried that my public criticism of the Board of Managers would block me from a more supportive role in the operation of the school. I knew better than most that the Board of Managers had a history of silencing anyone who disagreed with them. But I finally concluded that a Milton Hershey School without trust, fairness, and transparency would not be worth supporting. So I went public with my concerns about the abuse of power by the board, the violation of Mr. Hershey's trust, and the decline in standards for our Spartans.

The biggest alumni concern was that the mission of serving the neediest children was being abandoned. The students being recruited and enrolled were less needy (some came from families that were 150 percent above the poverty level), and they were also more academically qualified. Basically, children from lower-middle-class homes with the highest grades and fewest behavioral challenges were now deemed the most attractive candidates for admission. Instead of being a substitute home, the school was giving its kids more and longer holidays, including the entire summer at their family home. The students were also getting more material goods. Some of the more enterprising kids were selling items like laptop computers as fast as they received them.

Even as the school was being more generous, the students were being asked to do far less. They were no longer required to perform chores, even basic housekeeping chores like dusting and lawn mowing. The new laxity created problems at the school and eventually led to a houseparent protest, a real protest march, over the lack of discipline and security in the homes. This protest stunned the community and spoke to the deterioration of culture at the school. Although the school budget had doubled and the endowment had ballooned to $5 billion in six years, fewer students were being served. The changes being made seemed more about the optics of making the school look good than about fulfilling Mr. Hershey's mission of rescuing the neediest children.

Tomorrow I would assume command of a ship that seemed to have veered frighteningly off course. I never questioned my will to take on this task, but I did worry about whether I possessed sufficient skill to return the ship to its course. My honest self-inventory concluded, "Maybe." While I had taught briefly at a boarding school in Massachusetts and earned a master's degree in education at Johns Hopkins after majoring in psychology at Princeton, I was far from a typical educator. But I felt an obligation to do whatever I could and reasoned that maybe a different kind of leader was required to deal with such a unique challenge. My commitment and loyalty to Milton Hershey School was unconditional.

I had spent most of my professional career helping Fortune 1000 executives build high-performing management teams. Building a strong team that will last requires the creation of a corporate culture rooted in a clear, compelling vision and rock-solid values that define the behavior of the workforce. "You got to move your hips like you move your lips," we implored CEOs. That vision and those values needed to be absorbed and incorporated into the behavior of senior managers every day. That would be my blueprint for Milton Hershey School.

As I thought through the challenge I faced, I asked myself, Isn't that what the off-course, demoralized Milton Hershey School family needed? Far more than, say, strengthening the math curriculum, what the staff and children craved was old-fashioned straight-talk, genuine inclusion, and pride in returning to the founding purpose of this remarkable place.

It was clear that Milton Hershey School needed to keep pace with the times if it was to serve its students well. Primarily as a result of societal pressure, the school had expanded admissions to include girls and minority-group members. And the nature of poverty had radically changed since Milton Hershey's time. In the school's first decades, children ended up at the school often because of some sort of tragedy. Frankie and I were told that both our parents had been killed in a terrible automobile accident (the truth turned out to be far more horrific). Our relatives could not afford to take us in. And there were few resources available then to relatives who assumed the care of orphaned children. Other boys had alcoholic parents, had lost a father in the war, or had lost parents to a fire or some other tragedy.

The definition of "orphan" in the original deed of trust was "a boy without a father." In this sense, Milton Hershey was an orphan given his father's protracted absences. The definition eventually was broadened to include children who had lost either parent or who were "social orphans," defined as needy children of a single parent or divorced parents. By the time I returned, the face of poverty was increasingly that of a single mother or a grandmother.

Back in 1909, Milton Hershey envisioned his school for white orphan boys as a place where children with limited options would be properly raised and would learn a trade so each could grow into a self-reliant adult and be a good citizen. In 1909 very few people went to college or university, and it was a rare son of a poor or working-class family who would even entertain such ambitions. The lucky kids learned a trade or skill and went to work. Hershey Industrial School became renowned in the Mid-Atlantic region for the quality of the tradesmen it produced. Employers would flock to the high school in the spring time seeking young men who had manners, a strong work ethic, solid vocational training, and nowhere to go.

Throughout much of the school's history, the trustees and school administration almost reflexively resisted change. It is far easier to run a large institution and keep order by limiting innovation and flexibility. By sticking to rigid rules, such as the practice of having the boys milk cows twice a day every single day, the institution operated smoothly. But the regimentation sapped children's souls and spirits. I had felt both the comfort and the stifling oppression of uniformity for more than five thousand days as a HomeGuy. The milking program in particular remained for years a stark symbol of a resistance to modernization and change.

By the turn of the twenty-first century, it was clear that higher education was the key to success for many children. The old manufacturing base in the United States was largely gone. Those who achieved great career success usually were college educated. The Milton Hershey School curriculum needed to reflect that reality to best prepare its children for the future they would experience. At the same time, some of our kids would never go to college. We were again enrolling children who were not only emotionally traumatized but who also had serious academic and IQ limitations. Offering many of them the chance to master a vocation still made sense. Our diverse population of needy children would require a more customized approach going forward.

For the previous nine months, I had been acting president of the school. The appointment had been viewed as interim when I was asked to take the job, but I was constitutionally incapable of being a mere caretaker. I knew that I risked any chance at a permanent appointment by pressing for immediate change, but I felt compelled to act from day one. Despite my activism, or perhaps because of it, I got the permanent job. To me, being named president of Milton Hershey School the next day would be the greatest honor a human being could possibly receive.

After visiting the cemetery and paying tribute to my saviors, I drove the long way up to the Hotel Hershey around what us ol' timers still called Old Senior Hall. Mr. Hershey built this state-of-the-art school for his boys on the dominant peak overlooking the valley where he built his chocolate factory and the charming village for his employees. The building is enormous. It looks like an ancient castle, and each time I stand in front of it and look down into the valley, I am struck by Milton Hershey's choice of this site for the school. It tells me he wanted nothing but the best for his boys, including the proudest perch in the whole valley.

My inauguration took place at Founder's Hall, a towering structure with a marble rotunda and Austrian crystal chandeliers. The domed building, built at a cost well in excess of $25 million in the late 1960s, sticks out like an incongruous jeweled palace on the rolling rural campus of the orphanage. One of my predecessors erected this enormous and ostentatious structure to honor Milton Hershey. Like nearly all HomeGuys, I suspect Mr. Hershey would have viewed it as inappropriate. He abhorred waste and self-puffery. But at least its auditorium was big enough to hold the entire student body. On this day, September 14, 2003, Founder's Hall Auditorium was filled to capacity with more than 2,600, a crowd that included students, staff, alumni, and friends.

I stood at the top of the aisle at the rear of the massive auditorium listening to the buzz of the crowd. I could feel the excitement and hope. My mind was flooded with memories of my days at the Home and especially thoughts of my brother Frankie. I looked up to my older brother when I was a little boy. He protected me as much as one fragile child can protect another. But he was overwhelmed with fighting for his own acceptance and survival as he faced the "big guys" in a barnyard jungle that grew worse when he started junior high. Frankie was one of those boys who simply fell through the cracks. He was too different and too sensitive, and he had too many problems for a rigid institution like Milton Hershey School. Even though Frankie was older than me, I came to feel responsible for his welfare. He seemed to attract teasing and bullying like honey draws bees. I sensed his vulnerability. From that experience I acquired an antenna for children who are "different."

As I stood alone at the rear of the auditorium surrounded by the murmuring crowd, I thought of Frankie and all the other children who needed a special hand to steady and support them. I knew I had to help those kids. The magnificent Founder's Hall organ filled the hall with a deep, melodious sound that was soul shaking. The usher signaled me to begin my walk to the stage for the formal installation. As I took the first steps, the organist began to play the first chords of "When Johnny Comes Marching Home Again," the Civil War anthem of hope and a joyous homecoming.

> When Johnny comes marching home again
> Hurrah! Hurrah!
> We'll give him a hearty welcome then
> Hurrah! Hurrah!
> The men will cheer and the boys will shout
> The ladies they will all turn out
> And we'll all feel gay
> When Johnny comes marching home.

Goosebumps erupted on my arms as the crowd roared, but my thoughts remained with Frankie. My eyes filled with tears. Some of my friends also wept. "We're back, Frankie," I said to my dead brother. "And we'll make this good place better for kids like you."

Johnny and Frankie were marching home again. Hurrah! It was time to get to work.

2

ABANDONED

Johnny (left) gets his very own coat. *Courtesy of the Milton Hershey School*

I cannot pretend to be a dispassionate observer about the fate of Milton Hershey School. Everything about the school is intensely personal to me. When Frankie and I were deposited at what was then Hershey Industrial School in 1947, we experienced the good and the bad right away. The school took us in and provided us with new clothes, healthy farm food, and a roof over our heads. But we were also subjected to bullying by older boys and a level of institutionalization that seared me to the core. I feel the reverberations of those experiences to this day.

As the new president of Milton Hershey School, I had a big job to do. I had to simultaneously recapture the can-do traditional spirit and unique Spartan culture but do it in a way that would help our children thrive in a modern world that was radically different from that of my childhood. I could not let nostalgia cloud my judgment or govern through my personal stories. At the same time, my own unique experience informed my agenda. Let me tell you about my journey.

It is difficult to accurately re-create the memories of very early childhood. At the youngest ages, the fears and fancies of youth blur reality. But some images and events are so traumatic that they endure.

My first vivid memory ever is the day one of my mother's sisters took us on a very long drive through the Pennsylvania countryside. To me, a boy who would still qualify as a toddler, the trip seemed endless. It took four hours to travel more than one hundred miles. The car eventually pulled up next to a huge cottage that seemed to be overflowing with dozens of boys, something like an image from the nursery rhyme the *Old Woman Who Lived in a Shoe*. Boys were everywhere. But it did not feel like a magical nursery rhyme. Given our few and sheltered years, all the noise and activity overwhelmed us. While our aunt talked to a man one of the boys called "Pop," we clung to her legs, recoiling instinctively from the swirl of motion and the shouts of dozens of boys at fierce play.

Pop distracted us with a game called "Monkey in the Middle." Frankie was the monkey. Another boy and I tossed a ball back and forth, past Frankie. It was easy to keep the ball away from Frankie. Even at that age, he was awkward and sluggish in his movements. He tired of the game pretty quickly and walked back to where Pop was standing.

Our aunt was gone.

I had never before seen Frankie's eyes bulge that wide.

Pop was calm when he told us, "Your aunt said goodbye. They had to get on the road before nightfall. You'll be staying with us awhile and we'll take good care of you." I still remember frantically looking around for my aunt or anyone or anything remotely familiar. I felt completely alone. Frankie must have felt worse. He began to cry.

A big roly-poly kid named Gerald yelled, "Cry baby! The new boy is a cry baby!" He got a few kids to take up the "cry baby" chant until Pop grabbed him by the ear real hard. We trailed after the other thirty or so kids and somehow got through supper and then into neighboring cots with four older boys in a bedroom. We welcomed the "lights out" at first but the darkness quickly became scary. Frankie began to whimper and I joined in. Our hands reached out to one another to bridge the short divide between the cots. We knew that we could not be heard crying again on our very first day. Somehow we had to put up a brave front before all these larger boys.

Children have an instinctive understanding of the law of the jungle that rules in the childhood environment. We squeezed hands and stifled our sobs without having to say a word. As we silently cried ourselves to sleep, I felt again that cold empty feeling, a deep hollow pain. I did not yet know the word, but I truly felt abandoned.

That devastating feeling of abandonment was one experienced by nearly every child enrolled at the school. At that time it was a school for true orphans, so by definition all of us had lost at least one parent. Children do not truly understand the conditions that tear them away from their parents. In our case, the school told Frankie and me that our parents had been killed in an awful car accident. We did not realize that they had decided to lie to protect us from the terrible truth. Our Snow Shoe, Pennsylvania, relatives bought in on the deceit, and we never seriously questioned the adults or authorities who we thought cared for us. Once abandoned, we felt a gnawing sense of loss that eroded our basic sense of worth. And our dependency was complete.

For my brother and me, Hershey Industrial School delivered one remarkable experience after another in those early days and weeks. An ear-rattling fire alarm woke us the following morning. It would wake me up nearly every morning of my childhood. A fire alarm sounding in short bursts is a brutal but efficient way to wake up a household of more than thirty orphaned children in eight different rooms. I came to understand that institutions automatically revert to the most efficient course of action regardless of the options. That alarm was an early sign of efficiency in lieu of a kinder and gentler way to rouse sleeping children.

The routine never deviated at the cottage called Caaba: up at 7 a.m. for light chores and breakfast; change from house clothes to school clothes at 8 a.m. and be in class all day long with the same teacher except for gym; back to Caaba for a glass of milk; finish more chores and play for two hours; eat supper at 6 p.m.; do homework or read until 8 p.m.; lights out soon after. On Saturday we might play a game against another cottage or, once in a blue moon, watch the big Spartans play football. On Sunday, we always went into Hershey for Sunday Worship Service at the Hershey Theatre. Year in and year out, the routine never deviated.

We would quickly learn that there were house clothes, play clothes, school clothes, and "Sunday best" for worship service. On my first day at Hershey Industrial School, I leapt into my clothes, made a quick stop at the toilet, and raced down the hall until Miss Pincer, an aide to our houseparents, barked, "No running allowed, new boy!" The aroma of bacon greeted me even before I reached the kitchen door. Mom Arbogast and Miss Hartman, the other aide, were tending something over the stove.

They called out, "Good morning, Johnny and Frankie!"

"Good morning," we sheepishly replied.

Mom Arbogast welcomed us to breakfast. She always said that they made the best breakfast in central Pennsylvania. In fact, she said, "Mr. Hershey requires that we serve wholesome food and meat with every meal!" My stomach was already thanking God for this smart man.

Houseparents were exactly what the name implies: surrogate parents to the children assigned to their particular house. They were supposed to do everything a regular parent would do, from discipline to training in table manners. Some were wonderful; others fell substantially short of the ideal. Frankie and I got lucky. The Arbogasts were kind, generous, and loving. We could not have had better people care for us if our own parents could not do the job.

Later that morning, we were fitted for shirts, pants, and a new jacket from an enormous building called "the clothing room." That afternoon, we were amazed to see all our new clothes hanging in a shared closet. I had never seen my name on an item of clothing before. I beamed when I saw they had spelled "Johnny" correctly. Mom Arbogast opened our small dresser to reveal perfectly folded and stacked underwear, undershirts, pajamas, and socks. She embraced us together in a double hug and explained this was how drawers were kept at Caaba, our new home. The hug was kind, warm, and reassuring. The new clothes were really nice; the tidy drawer a gentle introduction to the Hershey Way. Rougher introductions to the Hershey Way were about to follow.

After supper, we all played in a huge gymnasium in the basement of the house. Each one of the cottages housing the youngest Hershey orphans had a gymnasium. It was a way for kids to let off steam in a controlled environment and a clear reflection of the founder's desire that his boys always have a good place to play. The play was rough and tumble, but it was unmatched by a frightening bedtime ritual that followed.

Our first group shower with thirty strange kids was an early indication of the regimentation that an institution follows to maintain standards and keep order. The kids raced for the shower room at the end of that first full day at the orphanage. Frankie and I, a little nervous about this group shower thing, lagged behind. We were uneasy about being naked in front of strangers. In the shower room, the other boys flung their house clothes into assigned cubby-holes but instead of heading to the shower, they each lined up in front of Pop Arbogast. Each naked boy held up his white jockey shorts for Pop's visual inspection.

Frankie and I were quite desperate to fit in and not draw undue attention to ourselves. We did not want to disappoint our houseparents, the adults we instinctively understood who were now our protectors. But inspecting underwear while we stood there stark naked? Why? What was he looking for? We moved cautiously to the end of the line. Frankie kept his underwear on, and I whispered to him that he was the only one not following the rules. He vowed to keep his shorts on as long as he could. I watched the inspection as each boy opened his underwear to Pop Arbogast who said things like "OK" or "Good" or "Brown streaks—two demerits" or "Brown and yellow streaks—three demerits." He made notes on a clipboard.

I suddenly realized what the inspection was about and quickly looked inside my undershorts. The unmistakable brown smears were as obvious as a skunk on a snow field. There was nothing I could do. When Pop reached me, he lowered his voice and said, "Brown streaks, Johnny, but we will let it go this first time. I will have a talk with you and Frankie." Frankie stood by me, shivering, crying, and still in his underwear.

Pop took us away from where Gerald and another boy were throwing taunts our way. Pop taught us all kinds of things about hygiene that night. We learned to double-fold toilet paper, how to wipe properly, and how to wash ourselves thoroughly. He told us this was very important because we had not been circumcised. I had no idea what that meant and wondered if there was something terribly wrong with us.

The hygiene lesson proved to be deeply embarrassing. I still remember that painful, hot feeling of acute embarrassment that burned down into my very bowels. I vowed to never experience that feeling again. But I would. Institutionalization tends to put a low priority on personal space and human dignity.

We survived our first full day, but inevitably it was the embarrassing moments that came back most vividly to both of us that night. I cried myself to sleep again holding my brother's hand. The last sounds I heard before drifting into unconsciousness were his whimpers.

> It is nighttime and we are outside. I can't see faces clearly, but the voices are loud and angry. Then I hear loud deafening noises, like fire crackers, followed by a flash of light and the smell of smoke. There is silence for a moment, and then screams rip through the air. People are yelling and rushing around. I see what I think is blood. I hear crying, including my own.

Screaming a muffled "Mommy! Mommy!" I awoke with a start to the four silent walls of a large bedroom with five other cots filled with sleeping boys. One sleeping lump responded to my cries with a groan and a rollover. Even Frankie did not wake. All I could think of was getting help. Something very bad had happened. I needed help. I felt too terrified to move but forced myself to move toward Frankie. But instead of waking my brother, I headed out the doorway and down a dimly lit hallway. I realized I was looking for Pop Arbogast, but nothing looked the same in the dark.

Trying my best to muffle my sobs, I turned right and ended up in the living room. I double-backed down another hall in search of the Arbogasts' apartment. They had their own small apartment in the same building that housed all the boys. I was lost. I felt panic welling up and began to pound on a closed door as hard as I could with my tiny fists.

A door behind me opened and I jumped. I had been knocking on a closet door. Pop Arbogast held out his arms and I instinctively ran into them. He soothed me. He seemed to know immediately that I had a bad dream. I clung to him as he walked me to a sofa. I heard Mom Arbogast's voice ask what was wrong. Pop said the new boy, Johnny, had a bad dream.

Pop asked me to tell him about my dream. I described the loud noises, the light flashes, the smoke, the screaming, but I did not know what was going on. Pop told me that everyone had dreams and he had some doozies of his own. He told me about one of his that featured scary fire-breathing dragons. It did not sound as real as mine but it calmed me down, and he walked me back to my bedroom.

I fell back asleep but shortly afterward I became aware of a sensation as terrifying as the dream: a warm wetness spreading from my pajama pants to my stomach. I had wet my bed before, but at home Mommy fondly excused the "little accident" and assured me I would grow out of it soon. But how would I survive this horror, this humiliation here? What would I do with my soaked sheets and stinking pajamas? Where would I get clean sheets? What about the mattress? What would the boys say? And the roly-poly kid, Gerald! And Pop Arbogast?

That morning, I had just enough time to pull the bedspread up to cover most of my mess when Pop approached. He sent me off to clean up and have breakfast and told me to make the bed later. As I left, he grabbed the top of the bedspread and pulled it all the way up. I did not know then that this perceptive man was way ahead of me. Pop Arbogast eventually figured out a way to hide my bedwetting by assigning me and a few others the "chore" of double-checking the bedrooms after everyone cleared out for breakfast. No one knew the chore gave us a chance to remove and rinse soiled sheets and pajamas and replace them with clean ones. I suspect he made up that chore to give me cover because he likely knew the cause of my night terrors. But he never let on.

Mom Arbogast had those sheets in the laundry before we finished breakfast. Mom and Pop Arbogast acted as our surrogate parents until each of us finished fifth grade at about the age of ten or eleven and moved on to the farmhomes for older boys. The Arbogasts were fair and kind. The affection and sensitivity they showed to a traumatized child made a crucial difference in the quality of my life and in my survival at Hershey Industrial School. The school did not allow kids to visit their former houseparents once they moved on to the farmhomes. The reason given for this was something about "avoiding unhealthy attachments," which was code, I later learned, for "houseparent conflict." But I never forgot the Arbogasts or their kindness.

Chores were a basic element of our daily ritual. Mr. Hershey had made it a condition of his deed of trust that his boys be trained in the "habits of industry." We spent our first waking hour groggily mopping floors, which were immaculately clean, and dusting furniture, which did not have a speck of dust. After school, we hopped with both feet on the bottom halves of cut-off trouser legs and did an early exuberant version of the Twist, years before it was invented, to shine the already sparkling linoleum floors. I loved floor shining. I would pretend to be carrying a football for the Spartans, evading tacklers as I slid around the shiny kitchen floor on the makeshift shiners. I did not like mopping, dusting, and sweeping. And washing and drying nearly forty sets of dishes was absolutely painful. However, the sense of responsibility that daily chores created and the feeling of accomplishment when they were done well helped to mold my character. I never forgot that either.

Gerald, and this was not his real name, remained a daily threat to me and my brother. We maintained constant vigilance. Like all bullies, Gerald sensed Frankie was more vulnerable than me, even though Frankie was the older sibling. Frankie was a gentle soul who took to heart Gerald's taunts. Each of us avoided him as much as possible. Children left to their own devices often revert to a primal pecking order that boosts the strong and assertive and oppresses the weak and vulnerable. Many of the children at Hershey had emotional challenges, although we did not really understand that at the time.

The cottages, like Caaba, held up to three dozen boys each between the ages of three and eleven. That is too many children for a houseparent couple and two aides to monitor at all times. The discrepancy in ages between the youngest and oldest also made the situation ripe for exploitation. Gerald, a classic bully, tormented Frankie and beat him up several times. He once bloodied Frankie's nose while the rest of us engaged in a fierce snow-ball fight with a neighboring cottage. He tried to drown me in the school swimming pool one day. Our gym teacher reached me just in time. He grabbed Gerald by the back of the neck and kicked him straight to the principal's office using his knee to whack Gerald's backside. I took great delight in Gerald's high-pitched squeal of protest in what was a rare moment of justifiable vengeance.

On our first day of school, Frankie was entering first grade and I was starting half-day kindergarten. We followed a herd of about thirty-six supercharged boys who moved like a pack of hungry dogs toward the school house. Our school was in a beautiful stone building. I slowed down to take a better look and noticed Gerald drifting toward us. I quickened my pace and urged Frankie to do the same. I sensed correctly that there was safety in numbers. As we moved away, Gerald began to shove Frankie on the shoulder. Before I had a chance to help my brother, another boy got between Gerald and Frankie and barked out, "Not today. You're not going to ruin their first day of school!" It was Eddie, an older boy who would prove to be a guardian to us.

Then I heard one kid mutter, "It's Hagy." He was referring to Mr. Hageman, part gym teacher, part disciplinarian, and all-powerful tyrant of Fanny B. Hershey Elementary School. He stood in the plaza outside the red brick school house like a sentry, nabbing any kids who defied his ban on running and yelling. Two boys he had collared were being bumped up the steps with high knee-jabs into their buttocks as he muttered, "Back-a-my knee running, back-a-my-knee talking" until he bumped them through the big front door.

The first thing I noticed about the school was the sharp, lemony scent that hung in the broad hallways, which branched out in many different directions. A short and stern-looking woman stood in the main hallway like a traffic cop. She was Miss Harm, the principal of Fanny B. When she spotted us, she smiled and her eyes lit up. She welcomed us and introduced us to our teachers: Mrs. Smith, the first-grade teacher for Frankie; and Miss Walker, for me. I was immediately dumbstruck. Miss Walker was the prettiest lady I had ever seen—well, next to my mother, whose visual image was fading fast.

From that moment on, my purpose in life was to please Miss Walker. I knew I wanted to please her as much as I wanted to continue breathing. There were boundless opportunities to please Miss Walker. Sometimes all it took was to get to my seat on time and be quiet and attentive. Because I desperately wanted her to call on me, it was often hard to raise my hand politely and wait to be called. I loved her classroom contests: alphabet bees and numbers games, which also gave me the chance to distinguish myself and prove worthy. The kids teased me for being a teacher's pet and for being in love with Miss Walker, but I paid them no mind. It was true blind adoration. Psychologists would call it *transference*. I transferred my yearning and love for my absent mother to this lovely, kind teacher.

In our first few years, Frankie fared well in the classroom but he could never keep up with the rest of us in the gym and on the playing fields. He proved too gentle for our rough-and-tumble games, including a free-for-all game we called "Get the B." Our houseparents thought *B* meant "the ball" but we all knew it meant "the bastard with the ball." As many as thirty of us would pounce on the poor boy who was stupid or brave enough to grab whatever we were using for a ball that day. Athletic ability has long separated boys and men throughout history, and Hershey Industrial School was no exception. Fortunate in my physical gifts, I quickly emerged as one of the better athletes in my age group.

I gravitated toward other boys who were just like me. Dick "Percy" Purcell and Carmen Gilotte became my new best friends. They lived in different houses: Percy at Granada and Carmen at Kinderhaus. Each of us was the best athlete in our respective houses. Throughout my time at Hershey, sports and competition would prove to be critical in molding my character and as an outlet for my anger, frustration, and loneliness. I could lose myself in the physical competition of sports and often did.

Having the huge gym in the subbasement of our cottage channeled the almost limitless energy of growing boys. We called it the "dungeon." It ran the entire width of the cottage and held a basketball court and storage rooms. It could have handled one hundred boys. All Pop Arbogast needed to do was yell "Gym time!" and roll out a few balls to divert all of us in intense play.

The gym also hosted our most sacred activities. Every December, about ten days before Christmas, a huge Christmas tree was put in the middle of the gym. Back in less-affluent times, Christmas had special significance for children, even those of intact families, because it was the one time when they might receive gifts. We orphans were no exception. We had so little in the way of family life and material goods that Christmas held even more meaning for us. All holidays at our Home were highly emotional. Most of us had some living relatives, and Christmas and other holidays were the times when we might be allowed visits from them. Those who did not receive visits—like the O'Brien brothers—felt anew the sting of rejection. The toxic combination of high expectations and fears played out in the weeks preceding major holidays with runaways, fights, and even a spike in underwear violations. Christmas, however, held a special place.

Some houseparents went to amazing lengths to maintain holiday calm. Each December, the Arbogasts transformed our gym into a Christmas wonderland. Our tree in Caaba was so big that it took two days for the biggest kids to help Pop decorate it. All around the walls of the gym, extending out from that towering Christmas tree, thirty-two boxes were marked on the floor in colored chalk, one for each boy with his name, like parking spaces for cars.

These personalized spots were where Pop would place our presents on Christmas Eve. Frankie and I decided to share one spot because it would look like we received more presents than we actually had on Christmas morning.

In the weeks leading up to Christmas, presents from relatives would arrive in brown shipping paper and be stored in our houseparents' apartment. The wait was agonizing; the packages, enticing. Singing carols on Christmas Eve just seemed to be another ploy to prolong the agony for one last night. It seemed endless. Our hopes for that special gift were boundless. On Christmas morning, Pop would make us wait at the top of the gym railing so we could "take in the magnificent sight" as we nearly leaped out of our skins with anticipation, bouncing in place like boxers readying for a match. Then he unleashed a tsunami of excited boys who swamped the gym floor in a sea of toys, wrapping paper, joy, and tears.

Christmas morning was a defining moment. It was not really about toys or getting something special. It was about being loved and wanted. Did our families care enough about us to buy us any presents and did they know enough about us to buy stuff we would like? Those were the questions. Our very sense of self-worth was wrapped up in those Christmas gifts.

Houseparents monitored the Christmas mail and would provide gifts for the boys who received little or nothing. It did not fool any of us, of course. The school gifts were all wrapped in Christmas paper instead of the brown mailing paper required by the U.S. Post Office. And the school gifts were pretty dorky. Instead of Slinkys or police cars or Erector Sets, the school gifts were mittens, fruit boxes, or stationery: the sort of presents you might give an elderly shut-in at a nursing home. The kids who received their fourth consecutive pair of mittens from the school were heartbroken.

When I look back on my childhood at Hershey Industrial School, there are moments that remain as clear as a perfectly cut diamond. One Christmas, for example, Frankie and I had six packages in our joint pile in the gym. We always saved the O'Brien gift for last because we understood that the "best" present would come from our most well-to-do relatives. Grandma Carlson sent us a package of assorted nuts, a Bible with pictures that Frankie wanted, and a jump rope for me. Gee whiz, I already had a jump rope. Aunt June sent us puzzles. I was not a big puzzle fan: too slow, too long, and too boring for me. All our hopes rested with the final present. Frankie had asked for a battery-powered ambulance with siren, back doors that opened with a stretcher, a nurse, and a few fake patients. I wanted a shiny black-and-gold police cruiser with flashing lights and siren. Yes! Our final box contained two vehicles: but alas, one was a taxi cab and the other was a measly old gasoline truck. It was not what we wanted; not even close. Frankie began to cry.

The discrepancy in gifting was painfully obvious on Christmas morning in the size of the piles of presents. One boy got a huge pile of gifts and a rocking horse nearly as big as he was. Next to him, were two fourth-grade twins who never received anything from relatives. One of the twins was throwing a school fruitcake against the cement gym wall and cursing it and the school. His brother looked like he was going to pounce on the boy with the big pile of gifts. When I look back at those moments as an adult, the pain of the disparity cuts me even sharper than it did at the time.

In the hierarchy of an orphanage, children with relatives who care about them have more status. Most of us understood, at some level, that we were throw-away children. The regard of others, particularly adults, was intrinsically tied to our self-esteem. No one talked about the importance of self-concept in children in those days. Indeed, such a concern would have been disparaged as coddling. Children were most definitely not to be coddled back then. Spare the Rod, Spoil the Child was still a well-regarded and often-voiced motto.

We were considered lucky boys and were often reminded of Mr. Hershey's benevolence and our good fortune. In those days, the notion of the worthy poor still prevailed. For example, this thinking deemed widows and children "worthy" of the benevolence of charity, but a man who suffered from alcoholism was considered unworthy. We, as children, were "worthy" so long as we behaved ourselves, kept ourselves neat and clean, and followed the rules. If we acted out, or deviated from the expectations for "good" children, then we could also fall out of favor and no longer be deemed deserving of the charity of the school.

For our first years at the school, Frankie and I never once got a family visit or left the school to visit our relatives. We did have family. Our maternal grandmother, Grandma Carlson, was a particular favorite:

a loving and kind woman who raised a dozen kids and simply could not raise two more grandchildren on her own. Aunt June and Uncle Ted, our mother's sister and brother, were also favorites, probably because they showed us the most attention. But my mother's youngest brother, Leroy, who was about our age even though he was our uncle, was a real playmate. Then there were our father's parents, Mimi and Byke O'Brien, who were our richest relatives. Our grandfather O'Brien drove a Cadillac and their house had a swimming pool. They could have taken us in, but they didn't want to. There was a pronounced coolness between the two families who lived on opposite sides of Snow Shoe that I never understood as a boy.

Hershey Industrial School had a philosophical approach to family visits back then: they disrupted order so they were discouraged and sharply limited. Evidently my brother and I were thought to be better off if we were allowed to adjust without interference from relatives, particularly when we were very young. Each Christmas, Frankie and I would go to the front foyer at the time visiting hours would begin and each year, Mom Arbogast would pull us aside and say, "Why don't you go down to the gym and play with your new toys?" Eventually, we understood the real message: No one is coming for you today; don't get your hopes up. Maybe no one will ever come.

In the summer, the boys with relatives could leave the school for a real vacation from Hershey for two weeks. We hungered to escape like inmates doing a life sentence at Sing Sing. Mom and Pop Arbogast tried to convince us we were too young to leave Hershey, but the passage of the years proved the lie when we saw lots of boys our age rejoining their families for a few weeks in July. The Arbogasts tried to make it up to us. They would take us special places, let us sleep in late, and even allow us to skip most of our chores.

But nothing could relieve that bone-marrow-deep pain of rejection. When the school emptied out in July, I felt more alone than at any other moment in my childhood. One year we actually packed our little black metal suitcases along with the other boys. Miss Pincer praised our packing as the neatest thing she had ever seen. We waited on the steps with our little suitcases all morning long while all but six of the thirty-two boys were embraced by relatives and driven away. It was painful to watch. Mom Arbogast tried to entice us away from the steps with offers of lunch, cookies, and even Hershey chocolate bars, the ultimate treat.

We refused to budge. We knew Snow Shoe was far away so it would take our relatives hours to reach us. We just knew our relatives were coming. Finally, as the shadows grew long across the driveway late that afternoon, we dragged ourselves and our much heavier suitcases up the staircase and into our bedroom.

We went straight to bed and shrugged off the Arbogasts' pleas that we eat dinner. We were exhausted from the loneliness. With most of the other boys away, we indulged in all-out sobs that night as we held hands and cried ourselves to sleep. I really missed being wanted.

That experience taught us something. Never again would we allow our hopes to go that high only to be sucker punched by disappointment. During our fourth year at the school, Frankie and I sought refuge in the toilets to avoid the sight of happy boys being scooped up by loving families for the summer break. Then we heard Pop's unmistakable steps coming down the hall. He called out that someone was there to see us. I thought who, what, what's the catch? Then he added, "Your family from Snow Shoe is here."

At those words, Frankie and I exploded from our adjoining stalls like the climax of a fireworks display, yanked up our pants, and ran headlong into Pop. He slowed us down long enough to tuck in our shirt-tails and smooth down our hair and walked us down the hall. Aunt June, Uncle Ted, and Leroy stood there. It was like the Coast Guard showing up to rescue drowning sailors. We were saved! Frankie and I had family that actually came for us. We were not the worst children in the universe or the most pathetic kids at Caaba. Someone cared!

Neither of us knew what to do. We barely knew these strangers. Then Uncle Ted swept me up in his long strong arms and said, "Johnny! You've gotten so big!" Aunt June hugged Frankie and told him how handsome he looked. Leroy acted as embarrassed as I felt.

A vacation meant we were "going over the wall." Running away or getting terminated from the school were the most extreme forms of going over the wall, but summer vacation trips counted as well. This was our first escape. An escape both frightening and exciting. I had no firm memories of Snow Shoe. I had been three years old the last time I saw it. It turned out that Mom Arbogast had secretly packed two small suitcases with new clothes for us. She did not want to raise our hopes by letting us pack our own clothing in advance. Our relatives had sent word they were coming but she remembered those years when no one had showed up and took the precaution to protect us from another crushing disappointment.

I quickly learned that there was a code of behavior among the HomeGuys. The older boys let us know what was expected of us. The first rule, which Frankie had frequently broken, was never cry and always stick up for yourself, even if that required fighting. The second rule was be loyal to one another. The houseparents, no matter how nice, were our keepers—as if we were in jail—and not to be trusted. The only people we could truly trust were one another. The third rule was never tell your own story of how you ended up at Hershey. Everyone had a bad story, and repeating it only rekindled the pain. We were also never to talk about "going home" or leaving; Hershey Industrial School was Home for us permanently, and the sooner we accepted that, the better off we would be.

Invariably this code came into collision with the adults who were responsible for us. When that happened, we were locked down in the gym for "serious sit-ins," as Pop called them.

One night right around Christmas, someone broke into Miss Pincer's apartment and stole some jewelry and money. We assumed we knew who the thieves were. Two of our number had gone over the wall the night before. But they were our brothers. We could not squeal.

We were called to the gym for a "serious sit-in," which required us to sit up straight on the concrete floor and not lean back against the wall. Pop sat on a hardwood chair and faced us. He reminded us that this wasn't any easier for him than for us, but we would sit there all night until someone told him the truth about the robbery. We sat from 7 to 9 p.m., our small butts getting sorer by the minute. No one talked. The clock inched past our bedtime. At 10 p.m. we were still sitting there, immobile, sworn to silence. Finally, Pop threw in the towel at 10:30 p.m. and sent us to bed but warned us we would be back on the floor after school the next day at 2:30 p.m. sharp. Fortunately, the boys who went over the wall were caught by police in their hometown the next day. They confessed and went to a juvenile detention center near Harrisburg.

I learned early that the sense of imprisonment at Hershey was nothing like the real thing. Juvenile detention was a real possibility for us unless we shaped up and followed the rules. As time passed, we became accustomed to the regimented life, and there was much about it, particularly for me as I grew into a student athlete, that would prove to be positive. Frankie and I came to understand that we were just two of many. We absorbed the lore of the school along with the ice-cold milk from our very own cows, the hearty farm fare of our meals, and the protective shelter of our formidable masonry structures. We may not have received cool Christmas gifts or cherished family visits, but we were indeed "fed with wholesome food . . . comfortably clothed . . . and fitly lodged," as Mr. Hershey decreed in his Deed of Trust.

3

THE FOUNDERS

The Founders: Milton and Catherine Hershey, 1910. *Courtesy of the Milton Hershey School*

From the beginning, Milton and Catherine Hershey viewed their charitable endeavor as more than a school. It was intended to be a refuge for its students; a substitute for the family and home so many of the children had lost. "These children must grow up with a feeling that they have a real home," is how Milton Hershey described the goal. The

Hersheys delivered on their promise. Those of us who lived at the school called it "Home" and referred to ourselves as "HomeBoys" or, more often, "HomeGuys." That was our reality.

The plight of the orphan was a concern of American society as early as Colonial times. The world was a harsher, crueler place then, particularly for the poor. Women routinely died in childbirth. Impoverished immigrants who had left their families far behind in places like Italy, Ireland, Germany, and Russia had no one in this country to turn to in times of need. Life expectancy for the average American man was forty-six years in 1900. Disease and accidents caused many premature deaths, leaving behind helpless children. In the late nineteenth century, orphan trains carried kids to the western and southern sections of the United States, and many children were sent to the country from city ghettoes to work on farms, essentially as free labor for the farm couples who took them in as foster children. The ad hoc safety net of the time was woven by churches, fraternal organizations, and a handful of very rich philanthropists: people like Milton and Kitty Hershey.

For the first half of his life, Milton Hershey focused his time and energy on making his fortune. He did not marry until May 25, 1898, a few months shy of his forty-first birthday. His bride was younger, twenty-seven years old, and from all accounts, Milton adored her. But it became painfully apparent after a decade of marriage that this union was not going to be blessed by children. Kitty suffered from chronic illness that eventually took her life at the tender age of forty-three.

Milton Hershey was not a man who accumulated wealth for its own sake. He publically stated and believed "it is a sin for a man to die rich." And Mr. Hershey vividly remembered the pain of his own dislocated childhood. His parents moved frequently, and his father was often absent. In some ways, he too was "orphaned." He attended seven different schools before his formal schooling ended at the age of twelve when he was apprenticed out to learn a craft. He and Kitty decided to provide to other young boys the security, opportunity, and community that he had yearned for as a lad. When an interviewer asked why he gave his entire fortune to orphan children, Mr. Hershey replied, "I have no heirs, that is, no children, so I decided to make the orphan boys of the United States my heirs."

The Hersheys were unquestionably influenced by the Progressive Era. Although the orphanages, almshouses, and work houses for the poor may have been well intended, the reality was far from ideal. By the turn of the twentieth century, there were hundreds of orphanages in the United States. Matthew Crenson, professor emeritus of political science at Johns Hopkins University, estimates that there were nearly one thousand orphanages with about 100,000 orphans. According to Professor Crenson, orphanages were highly regimented, harsh places. Some were run like prisons: children were dressed in uniforms, marched to meals, and ordered to eat in silence. Physical and sexual abuse were commonplace. This Dickensian bleakness came to the attention of the progressive reformers of the day. In January of 1909, the very year Milton Hershey created his school, President Theodore Roosevelt sponsored the White House Conference on the Care of Dependent Children. In his book *Building the Invisible Orphanage: A Pre-History of the American Welfare System*, Professor Crenson makes the case that the brutality of the orphanages exposed at this conference led to the mothers' pension, the forerunner of Aid to Families with Dependent Children (AFDC) and the modern welfare system.

From the start, Milton Hershey had a clear and practical vision for his school. He envisioned his school as a kind, nurturing, home-like environment for homeless boys but also as a trade school, a preparation for life, rather than a preparatory school for higher education. In 1910, U.S. Census data shows only 2.7 percent of the adult population of the United States held college degrees. In those rougher days, a boy needed to learn how to survive and support himself, so farming and the conventional craft trades were emphasized. It was not an era that coddled children. Life could be brutal and short, and children learned at an early age how to stand on their own.

While biographers say Milton Hershey acquired an appreciation for the finer things in life during his travels to Europe and Cuba after becoming a wealthy man, he remained at heart a modest, hardworking, sober man. He created an institution that would mold modest, hardworking boys; a simple home that would develop strong moral character and provide life skills for needy children.

While his formal education was limited, M. S. Hershey was clever and smart. Like many self-made men, he did not delegate authority easily. But he did due diligence to take advantage of the experience of others and to learn about the best practices of the day before he established his school. James D. McMahon Jr., director of the Milton Hershey School Department of School History, has done extensive research on the history of the school and has shared it with me. He told me that Milton Hershey was likely influenced by the nineteenth-century German educator Friedrich Froebel, who believed that children learned through play. Froebel created the first kindergarten. Hershey also consulted with the Russell Sage Foundation in New York, which had been founded just a few years earlier for "the improvement of social and living conditions in the United States," particularly for the poor and the elderly.

Since the Hersheys wanted their school to be among the best, they adopted the best practice of the time: a system of housing children with surrogate parents in cottages in lieu of the big, dormitory-style facilities of the past. Hershey spent many days at Girard College, a boarding school for "poor white male orphans" in Philadelphia, which had already been in operation for fifty years. And he followed the example of the founder of that school, the philanthropist Stephen Girard, in drawing up the deed of trust that created his school to guarantee that his school would remain faithful to his vision beyond his lifetime.

Stephen Girard, a French-born banker and philanthropist, made an interesting role model for Mr. Hershey. Girard was considered the richest man in America when he died in 1831. His Philadelphia bank saved the U.S. government from economic collapse during the War of 1812 by guaranteeing the wartime debt of the still-young country. Like the Hersheys, he was childless. His wife went mad and died in an insane asylum. When he died, his last will and testament left a bequest for creation of a Philadelphia boarding school. The orphanage opened in 1848 after a prolonged legal struggle between the city of Philadelphia and Girard's French relatives, who contested the will. The U.S. Supreme Court ruled in favor of the city based upon Mr. Girard's clear instructions. While confronted by serious financial challenge, the school exists to this day as Girard College, a forty-three-acre prep school in the heart of Philadelphia.

By drawing upon the legal lessons of the Girard Supreme Court case, Mr. Hershey could be reasonably assured that his vision would prevail into perpetuity. The deed of trust put authority into the hands of a small group of local men selected by Mr. Hershey. This was a deviation from Mr. Girard's school, which put power into the hands of local elected officials in Philadelphia and their successors. By Mr. Hershey's time, public corruption was endemic, so he prudently handpicked the original Board of Managers. The original trustees were close friends and business associates who reflected the establishment of the time. Hershey was the wealthiest man in a community that carried his name, so he clearly called the shots. But the original Board of Managers likely agreed with his approach, and they certainly agreed that he could do whatever he wished with his hard-earned fortune. These men included John Snyder, Hershey's lawyer who drew up the deed of trust; U. G. Risser, a local doctor; and John A. Landis, a local minister. Mr. Hershey knew the character of these men and knew they were "above reproach." When a vacancy occurred, the Board of Managers chose the new member.

During his lifetime, M. S. Hershey took an active interest in the school but he did not interfere with its operations. The founder did not know much about running a school or raising children so he relied upon professional educators who could implement his vision. From all accounts, he doted on his boys. He invited boys to come to High Point, his beautiful home, for special lunches and would set out tables on the expansive lawn. He often took visitors to see the boys. There are photographs from that time of Milton Hershey with his boys that show the founder's unquestioned affection for his HomeBoys. One of my favorites shows M. S. Hershey sitting with a cute tyke perched on his lap. Another photo shows him holding a young boy close to his heart. He attended graduation exercises nearly every year and personally shook the hand of and gave a diploma to each graduate.

After his death, the board kept on with the practice of filling vacancies with men just like them who shared Mr. Hershey's values and views. The board controlled term limits, and for many decades board members took no compensation for their service. Serving the school was viewed as reward enough. One of the last board members to serve with the founder was Arthur R. Whiteman. He enrolled at the age of four and went to work for the Hershey Trust Company at the age of fifteen. Like many school and trust leaders, he never left Hershey, and he served his home with distinction for the rest of his life. As a member of the class of 1927, he was the first alumnus to serve on the Board of Managers. His retirement in 1974 at the age of sixty-five broke the last direct tie between the founder and his board.

Mr. Hershey never saw the need for conflict of interest and account-ability measures, term limits, or any of the other governance conditions that are sadly needed and routine today in corporate America. He lived in an era when a man's handshake was all that was needed to seal a deal. He simply trusted his colleagues. I suspect he never considered what absolute power might do in the hands of ambitious and self-interested trustees generations later; that is, trustees with no direct connection to the founder and little understanding of his values or his vision. I came to see it as a fatal flaw of a mortal man who could not have foreseen the grave danger inherent in an all-powerful, self-perpetuating board so many years in the future.

The school began modestly with two sets of brothers: Nelson and Irvin Wagner, whose recently widowed mother was still nursing her third child (a widow with three young children faced a precarious exis-tence in those days); and Jacob and Guy Weber. By the end of the first school year, there were seventeen boys, all living at the Homestead, the birthplace of Milton Hershey. The Homestead had been built by Her-shey's great-grandparents, Isaac and Anna Hershey, who settled in Der-ry Township in 1796. Milton's grandfather sold the farm in 1867, but Milton bought it back at an auction in 1896. The Hersheys renovated and upgraded the Homestead for their temporary use during construc-tion of their permanent home in Hershey, a twenty-two-room mansion called High Point. By any estimation, High Point was a mansion, but by the plutocrat practices of the time, it was considered fairly modest. Completion of High Point allowed the entire Hershey Industrial School to operate out of the Homestead. The boys ate, slept, attended class, and did their chores in the old farmhouse.

The school grew faster than the Hersheys expected, and it became difficult to find meaningful work for all the students, particularly as the boys grew older. So in 1929, they placed the older boys, those in grades 6 through 12, on the dairy farms used to produce milk for the chocolate factory. Mr. Hershey felt strongly that growing up on a farm was ideal for children. He felt the boys would grow up in wholesome surround-ings, be close to nature, and learn to do productive chores on a farm. The rural ideal is one that runs throughout history, and Mr. Hershey viewed the bucolic setting as optimal for growing healthy boys.

During Milton Hershey's life and for about forty years after his death, the system worked pretty well. The board saw little need to tinker with a successful formula as the school continued to grow. Not surprisingly, enrollment tripled during the Great Depression in the 1930s. While Kitty and Milton had "dreamed of giving one hundred orphans a home," the enrollment surpassed one thousand by 1937. Upon seeing the exponential increase of destitute children, Milton amended the deed of trust to serve even more students. For the first forty years, boys were indentured to the school, legally contracted to comply with the rules and regulations of the institution until they turned eighteen. The indenture system dated back to Colonial times. To deal with a labor shortage in the Colonies, poor English men would sign contracts to work for a certain number of years to pay off their passage to the New World. It fell out of favor after the American Revolution and came to be viewed as a form of servitude, akin to slavery. The last student to be indentured was Charles S. Campayner, who came to the school two years after we did in 1949. By that time, the idea of putting boys into contractual servitude, no matter how benevolent, was considered wrong.

I have a copy of my own indenture contract. My grandmother signed away my youth on February 13, 1948. The indenture contract said that I would remain in the "exclusive custody and control" of the Board of Managers until I turned eighteen on November 27, 1961. The contract is brutally direct. It states,

> Said orphan [me] shall faithfully, honestly, and obediently serve the said Managers and conform to all their rules and regulations with reference to residence, studies, work and duty, and all other rules and regulations by the Managers, their executive officers, or others by them appointed; the intent of this release being to enable the Managers to enforce in relation to the said orphan every proper restraint, and to prevent relatives, friends, or others from interfering with or withdrawing the said orphan from the school.

If I misbehaved in any way, the contract made it clear the school could expel me on the spot. The Board of Managers had complete control over every aspect of my life.

Children naturally resist authority at different points in their development and rebel against parents and parental substitutes. As much as we rebelled against the constraints of institutionalization and acted out, as boys do, few of us would risk expulsion. Most of us came to understand we were lucky to be at Hershey Industrial School and would probably be worse off anywhere else. A "lifer" like me also had a hard time imagining being any other place. My limited visits to relatives in the summer did not displace my belief that Hershey Industrial School was Home. Even so, I dreaded giving up my relative freedom and a "real family" each time we prepared to leave Snow Shoe after a family visit with my relatives. Frankie and I literally begged our grandparents to "save us from the horrors of the institution!" But as the car neared Hershey, my heart would leap and I would eagerly anticipate being back with my friends, back Home. My mind was conflicted about my two homes, but my heart increasingly belonged in Hershey.

For much of the school's history, changes tended to be measured, controlled, and gradual. Hershey Industrial School's name was changed to Milton Hershey School in 1951, four years after I arrived. It coincided with the tenure of Superintendent John Hershey, who worked at the school for forty-two years. He and his wife began their career at the school as houseparents. He was a deft insider player and eventually became one of the longest serving leaders of the school. He was not related to Milton Hershey. Many alumni viewed Dr. Hershey, as we were required to call him, as a politician. He was a quintessential survivor who knew how to adjust to changing times, and he understood that the world was changing. The Baby Boom generation was being born. There were so many children born after World War II that the generation has had a disproportionate impact upon popular culture ever since. Dr. Spock, America's most prominent pediatrician, and other experts in the growing fields of sociology, psychology, and education had brandnew ideas about what was good for children and how children should be raised.

The debate about the best environment for growing children continues today. The foster-care system effectively took over the job of orphanages in modern times. I recognize that most children are best off being raised by their parents or relatives. But the children at Milton Hershey School were and are not typical. My own experience and years of observation have convinced me that this type of residential school is the best answer for many children whose parents are unwilling or unable to care for them. Not all kids will thrive at a school like Milton Hershey School, but for those who are suited, it can be transformative.

By the time the Russians launched Sputnik in 1957, the need for improvements in the education of the boys was obvious as the modern world began to demand more sophisticated knowledge of its workers. This was a departure from the Milton Hershey vision. Mr. Hershey did not think much of fancy college education. He had sent two Hershey Industrial School graduates to college in 1926 and 1927, and the experiment went badly. The first, Harold H. Sours, failed to adjust to college life after years at Hershey Industrial School and dropped out. The other boy was forced to drop out to care for a sick uncle. Mr. Hershey was reluctant to make further investments in college for his students after that, but he left the issue open for future reconsideration. He was not hostile to higher education. He created Hershey Junior College in the village, which many of the graduates of his school attended. In 1956, eleven years after his death, the Board of Managers created a college scholarship program. Even a Board of Managers with one foot firmly planted in the past recognized that economic changes were making higher education more important.

While the school clung to certain traditions—the dairy farms remained operational far longer than I considered necessary, for example—Dr. Hershey and the school administrators did make adjustments to conform to the child-rearing practices of the time. For example, the cottage homes with thirty or more boys were finally deemed too large for a real family-like experience and beyond the capacity of two houseparents to manage. So in the 1960s, John Hershey oversaw a building boom that resulted in sixty-three new student homes and the renovation of forty others. To make the residences more home-like, the number of students living in each house was limited to no more than a dozen boys. This was a substantial improvement from the twenty-four to thirty-two kids per house at my time. John Hershey's tenure also brought the first black-and-white television sets and upholstered furniture to the cottages. An Intermediate Division, which put students in grades 5 through 8 by themselves, was introduced in 1961, the year I graduated. This was a historic change that significantly reduced the conditions for bullying. In 1968 the deed of trust was amended to allow boys of other races to enroll, and then it was amended again to allow girls in 1976. The Spartan "bubble" remained intact, but the student body and student life became a lot more real.

With plentiful foster care and social safety-nets, the supply of legal orphans dwindled throughout the century, and in 1977, the first "social orphans" were admitted to Milton Hershey School. Social orphans are children whose parents are alive but unable to care for them. By the 1970s, the nature of poverty had changed: life expectancy had lengthened, and fewer children actually lost their parents to death. However, poverty had become more insidious, and children of poverty were often born into families that had been poor for generations. Multigenerational poverty brought a range of attendant problems from drug and sexual abuse to an undercurrent of persistent violence and few positive role models. The result: deeply vulnerable children, mired in a cesspool of poverty that few would ever be able to escape without a lot of help. Children in poverty in the twenty-first century faced an even bleaker future than poor kids of my generation.

While income has nothing to do with love or good parenting, it is clear that poor people live on the edge. People who live in poverty can barely pay a subsidized rent and feed their growing children. Others cannot afford to move out of a dangerous neighborhood where gangs and drug dealers recruit boys as young as nine and ten years old. The working poor often work two or more jobs and cannot be home enough to supervise young children. These parents and grandparents make an enormous personal sacrifice when they send their boys and girls away to Milton Hershey School. But most do it because they want their children to have better lives than their own, the age-old imperative of good parents.

While the modest changes introduced during John Hershey's tenure reflected some of the changes in education and child rearing taking place outside of Hershey, the school and the community surrounding it often seemed to be hermetically sealed like the snow globes popular in this town. Milton Hershey created a utopian village for his workers next to his enormous chocolate factory that mass produced the first affordable chocolate candies in America. He allowed them to purchase their own homes on tree-lined streets in the shadow of the largest chocolate factory in the world. Other manufacturers created housing for workers but rented the units. Mr. Hershey believed that workers would take more care of and feel a deeper connection and commitment to the town if they owned their own homes. He was right about that. He also believed in profit sharing. Hershey bonuses ensured a stable and largely content work force. He, like most manufacturers, experienced labor problems at the beginning of the organized-labor movement, and there were issues of discrimination involving recent immigrants from Italy. But those troubles proved to be a bump in the road. His compassion for his workers would eventually be repaid when the townspeople became a critical component of our alumni rebellion many years later.

The Board of Managers became even more isolated than the community. Charitable and other private trusts often operate independently with virtually no accountability. The Milton Hershey board was no exception to that general rule. It takes an extraordinary circumstance for the courts or government to interfere in a private charitable trust. As boys, we only caught a glimpse of the Board of Managers at commencement and other momentous occasions. We were unaware of their power. We mistakenly thought that the head of the school, our teachers, and our houseparents were all powerful. From our narrow perspective, they certainly held all the cards when they closed the doors of a student home or classroom. And the "Super," John Hershey, was the equivalent of a king. Little did we know that those prosperous board members in their dark suits who sat so impassively together at the graduation ceremony each spring at the Hershey Theatre were the ones who actually controlled every facet of our lives. In the careless and disrespectful way of boys, we called them the "fat cats."

Thanks to strong economic growth in the twentieth and twenty-first century, Milton Hershey's original $60 million endowment grew like topsy along with an enormous middle class with a taste for his candy bars. Even low-income folks could indulge themselves with a five- or ten-cent candy bar. Milton Hershey would never have dreamed of the astonishing financial success of his company in the decades after his death. The value of his iconic chocolate company grew and grew until it eventually was worth billions. That is billions with a *b*, and it grew into a Fortune 500 company, ranking among the largest in the United States. That staggering wealth and the questionable oversight of the Board of Managers contributed to the crisis that brought me back so many years later.

The financial structure of the school is highly unusual. There are four distinct entities. The Milton Hershey School Trust oversees the Milton Hershey School, which owns the Hershey [chocolate] Company, the Hershey Trust Company, and the Hershey Entertainment and Resort Company. The Hershey Trust Company is a private bank that holds, invests, and manages the billions of dollars in assets of the huge endowment that operates the school. The Hershey Entertainment and Resorts Company manages Hersheypark, Hotel Hershey, and a dozen other commercial ventures. The profits from these companies go into the trust fund for the school. The fourth board is the Board of Managers (same members as the trust board), the trustees who oversee the school.

When I was installed as president, the institution had been unsettled for more than a decade. Part of my job would be to restore a sense of equilibrium even as we made overdue changes and implemented the course correction the alumni wanted. It would not be easy. It is never easy to find the perfect balance between adherence to a time-honored tradition and pushing for the change needed to keep up with the times. But I felt I had a North Star to guide me: Mr. Hershey and his vision. I also had an advantage alien to most members of the Board of Managers. I had been a HomeGuy for my entire childhood. My experiences and those of Frankie and of all my HomeGuy brothers would guide my gut and intellect as we confronted these challenges head on.

4

BARNYARD JUNGLE

Barnguys . . . escaping house chores. *Courtesy of the Milton Hershey School*

An intense bond of blood, love, and shared fear tied me to my brother Frankie. The O'Brien brothers were an inseparable team; it was us against the rest of the world. Although Frankie was two years older, I sometimes felt like the older sibling. He was different: more fragile and sensitive than most other boys. He recoiled from the physicality of rough play that I relished. We each burned for approval and love and would do just about anything to win the praise of adults. While I would occasionally challenge authority and arbitrary rules, Frankie's instinct was to duck and hide. Yet I studied hard, played hard, and followed most of the rules. Frankie also did well when he had the emotional support and protection he so desperately needed. Unfortunately, he did not always get it.

The school was divided by age but not in a way that made much sense. We first lived in Caaba Cottage with thirty-two boys who ranged from toddlers through fifth grade. As soon as a boy finished fifth grade, he moved to one of the farmhomes where boys in grades 6 through 12 lived. The age disparity at Caaba was not too extreme, and bullying was only sporadic. Boys of that age are eager to please, and most of the older boys enjoyed showing the younger boys "the MHS way."

Going out to the farmhomes was just plain scary. Putting boys who were eleven together with boys who were nineteen was insane. At that time, the officials seemed oblivious to the way younger children could be exploited by older teenagers. There was also little sensitivity to the bonds between siblings and the importance of those connections. Frankie and I were allowed to bunk in the same room at Caaba, but once he went off to the farmhome, we rarely saw one another for two long years. Visits were limited to a spare thirty minutes in the middle of a field next to watermelons or tomatoes or rushed whispers after church services on Sunday. The Milton Hershey School administrators thought the older boys would corrupt the younger kids and did not want the younger boys to know too much about life on the farms. The school always knew best. We were constantly told that the rules and restrictions were "in our own best interests."

Frankie did not want to leave me or the Arbogasts. We had heard whispers about the big guys and the bullying. It hadn't been so long since Gerard had taunted him at Caaba. Frankie had thrived at Caaba once Gerard went off to his farmhome. To leave now when he was happy and doing so well was just heartbreaking for Frankie. He cried himself to sleep that last night. We reached out from our cots and clasped hands. The familiar ritual felt so solemn on our last night together that we could not even make eye contact. Our hands were still joined when I awakened to pee.

School rules prevented Pop Arbogast from taking Frankie to his new home at Spring Creek, Frankie's designated farmhome, even though Pop had promised to deliver him personally. Frankie would have to make the trip alone on the Mealbus. Years later, I marveled at the fact that my brother was less than a mile away from me. The distance might have been hundreds of miles, given the extraordinary isolation of our lives. While I could have walked there in a matter of minutes, my brother seemed to have moved to a totally different world.

The Mealbus was an ugly, brown, industrial truck with one seat for the driver. The truck bed contained racks on each side to hold stacked metal pots filled with several days of food for a student home. The open floor-space in the middle was filled with baskets of fruits, vegetables, and mail.

Frankie flew into a rage when the bus arrived. I had never seen my mild-mannered brother so out of control. I tried to hug him to settle him down but he flung me off as if I were a flea. The driver had to help Pop hold Frankie until he calmed down. It later occurred to me that Frankie had an almost animal-like, instinctive sense of the threat that awaited him at the farmhome. It was as if a domesticated bunny had been pried from its cage and tossed into a terrifying wilderness.

There is a huge difference in size, maturity, and sophistication between boys who are eleven and young men of eighteen or nineteen. My brother tried to protect me while I was still at Caaba by giving me very little advance knowledge of life on the farm. He did tell me that he did not like his new houseparents or most of his housemates. He said "some of the boys were mean to him." When he complained to his houseparents, they told him to stick up for himself and refused to protect him. But he urged me not to worry, and at the time, I was easily distracted by my friends and activities. Frankie's kind reticence gave me a gift of two additional stress-free years at Caaba, a slice of happy, carefree childhood. It is amazing that a child as young as Frankie could act so nobly to protect his brother.

As I was finishing up fifth grade I still suffered from that same vivid nightmare that had plagued my nights since I first arrived, but it came less often. However, with less frequency, came more detail. I now knew it had something to do with my mother and it took place at my grandparent O'Brien's house in Snow Shoe. Frankie had recently revealed some of the details from his own nightmares. We shared those nighttime traumas. When the nightmare jolted me awake with a start and a cry, I tucked myself into a ball and held onto my knees until my breathing slowed down and the tears stopped trying to flow. Crying, even in the dark, was simply no longer acceptable. As a ten-year-old boy, I was too big to be running down the hall in search of Pop Arbogast any longer. The school environment discouraged crying or any other unseemly show of emotion. Emotion disrupted order. It also tagged you as weak and vulnerable. I learned to stifle my true feelings and put on a mask that fooled everyone and eventually came to be my face to the world.

Frankie tried to convince me to go to another farmhome when the time came for me to graduate to the next level. He claimed it was because I would benefit from a house father who was more like a coach and not just a dairy farmer like Mr. Weaver, his house father. But I would not even consider being separated from my brother any longer. The two years had seemed like forever. I saw through his words and knew he was lying to protect me. So I finished fifth grade and joined Frankie at Unit 34, Spring Creek.

I packed up my possessions: a baseball glove, a few puzzles, and a Slinky. Everything fit into a small box. I did not take any clothes because I would be issued new clothing at Spring Creek. Looking around my bedroom at Caaba for the last time, I realized that the little cot, the tiny dresser, and the closet were the only things that had been truly mine for the past seven years. Now they would belong to another boy. It was wrenching to leave the Arbogasts who went so far beyond the call to care for me and to leave the place where I had lived longer than any other in my life. Wearing my favorite shirt covered with baseballs and bats and a pair of khaki pants, I stood tall on the Caaba porch and faced my future with all the confidence that a terrified ten year old could muster.

The Mealbus driver was a big, husky guy named Walt who had taken this journey himself in 1937 on his own trip from a cottage to a farmhome. He graduated in 1944. He told me that the farmhome life was much tougher and I "should watch my mouth and do what the big guys told me to do." He said he had stared down a bully once by standing up to him. That impressed me. I appreciated his advice.

From the start, my new houseparents, the Weavers, refused to call me by my name, Johnny. They already had a Johnny at the farm so they called me John. I thought it was a joke at first but it was clear they were dead serious. It made me feel even less significant and less alive than usual. Suddenly, I had more work to do to prove myself worthwhile. Refusing to call a boy by his preferred name or calling him "boy" was a severe form of depersonalization—a word I felt long before I ever read it in a college psychology textbook.

Mrs. Weaver told Frankie to show me our room and said he was to keep me from touching any of my new clothing. Our bedroom was slightly bigger than a closet; the two cots filled almost the entire room with a tiny space between them and a little room at the foot. The small size surprised me but I was delighted to be in a separate bedroom with my brother. And it was always a treat to get new clothes. As I remember it, I was pulling my new jacket out of the closet when Mrs. Weaver appeared at the door.

"Frankie! Didn't I tell you not to let John touch any of his new clothing?" she screamed.

Frankie cowered.

"That means detentions for you, boy," she shouted. "Get downstairs. I will deal with you later."

Frankie slinked away and I stood there befuddled. I was so confused. I thought they were *my* clothes. She made it emphatically clear that the clothing belonged to the school. "You kids come here with nothing and you expect everything. No wonder your families didn't want you . . . you don't appreciate . . ." she then stopped, apparently catching herself, and instructed me to put my box of possessions away and report to the kitchen in fifteen minutes.

The encounter left me shocked. What did she mean? Our families didn't want us? We expected everything? And weren't they *my* clothes?

Mr. Weaver was no Pop Arbogast. He was a large man of medium height with big shoulders and arms and a protruding pot-belly the size of a 1950s-era television set. He had a beet red face with a wart-dotted nose and exuded a strange odor that I later came to understand was the telltale scent of whiskey. He was as mean as his wife, but far more distant.

At supper that night, he ordered me to "set" right by him and called me John.

"My name is Johnny," I said.

"What is that? Are you speaking to me, boy?" he snarled.

"I said . . . they call me Johnny."

"Whoa. Hold it right there," Mr. Weaver roared. "You call me Sir or Pop, boy, if you be speaking to me. You got that?"

He referred to the farmhome as Unit 34 instead of Spring Creek. I was only beginning to understand what institutionalization meant. Calling student homes by numbers and letters, instead of lovely names like Spring Creek, Buena Vista, and Rosemont, was part of the systemic regimentation that defined my childhood. The strict behavior code based on merits, demerits, and detentions was another way to maintain order. Every second of every day was structured and controlled. Children do need structure, but that kind of oppressive regimentation can be soul crushing to a child who is creative or different or simply free spirited.

That first night, I had to pass a gauntlet of boys hooting and laughing at me in my new yellow pajamas as I went from the bathroom to our bedroom. Our bedroom was at one end of a long corridor; the bathroom was at the opposite end. As an adult, I eventually realized there were elements to the subculture at the industrial school that were similar to the hierarchy, hazing, and bullying that takes place in prisons. In an isolated environment, the small, young, and weak become prey for those who are bigger, stronger, older, and meaner. Mr. Weaver played the role of corrections officer: checking us in each night before light's out, and snapping orders to keep elbows off the table, to keep eyes on the plate, to only talk softly to people next to you, not to lounge on the furniture in the TV room, and not to speak to him in that tone ("Call me Sir, boy").

After just a few hours at Spring Creek, I was exhausted from the strange new kids, the mean housefather, the new rules, the unfamiliar rooms, and the scary housemother. Frankie said our tiny bedroom was our "sanctuary." He spelled the word for me. I liked the sound of it. Tucked into those little cots, we immediately joined hands as if we had not been separated for two years. In the dim light, I could see a broad smile spread across my brother's face. Good. I had rarely seen him smile since he left Caaba. I was weary from the mental acrobatics involved in adjusting to this new hostile environment and anxious about the future but happy to be with Frankie. Sleep was a sweet escape.

The next morning, the clang of an alarm bell outside our room, an alarm so loud the little room vibrated, woke me at 5:15 a.m. It was still dark. "The cows must be milked at this hour," Frankie explained as I complained. We made our beds, put on house clothes, and headed to the kitchen. Mrs. Weaver ordered Frankie to show me how to dust and mop the living room. I already knew how to dust, but Frankie demonstrated by carefully digging into corners with the dust rag and sternly warned me I had to do it properly to pass "inspection."

For inspection, Mrs. Weaver actually put on white gloves and ran one gloved finger over every surface; the baseboards, the window sills, the furniture. I was doing OK until she moved a large table wedged between the couch and the wall and triumphantly found a wad of hair and dust.

"You're not such a great cleaner after all, John," she snarled.

I was so taken aback, I started to stammer excuses. "No one said I had to clean under furniture, ma'am."

"All flat surfaces, John," she said. "Didn't Frankie tell you?"

"I don't think I could even move that couch and table. This isn't fair." Now I was whining.

"Don't you be talkin' back to me, boy," she hissed. "You never talk back to your superiors, you hear? Do you?"

When I said I would dust more, she barked that chores were over. I protested that the barn guys were not finished milking yet and insisted I could keep dusting.

"Chores are over when I say they are over!" barked the witch. "You, John, are going to miss your first Friday night town privilege for insubordination!" And off she went on her broom!

I did not even know what the word "insubordination" meant. But I was hurt and resentful that my first opportunity to go into town with my brother and the other boys would be denied so quickly and for such flimsy reasons.

These angry houseparents were nothing like the loving Arbogasts. They were dictators; passing edicts based upon their convenience and whim. One of the shortcomings in those years was the extraordinary discrepancy in the quality of houseparents. Some were kind and actually nurturing, but often the farm houseparents were great farmers but clueless about the needs of growing children. The Weavers fit into that category. Mr. Weaver may have been a great dairy farmer, but he was a poor parent substitute. His beleaguered wife, stuck in the house with dozens of rambunctious boys, took out her unhappiness on us. I eventually felt sorry for her.

I had to figure out how to survive. The boys were divided into two groups: the house guys and the barn guys. The barn guys were older and responsible for chores like mucking out the barns and milking the cows twice a day. The house guys did housework and cooking. Frankie was a house guy, and my age made me a likely house guy, but I knew I had to escape Mrs. Weaver's sharp tongue and eye. I figured it could not be worse in the barns, and even at that age, I was eager to be among the "big guys."

But before I could plot my escape I had my infamous encounter with the "mackey bowl." That Friday night, I hung out in the basement jealously watching my new brothers showering and getting ready to go into town—going over the wall. Miserable that I would not be going with them and still resentful over my punishment, I happened to run my hands over the bottom of a huge stone basin they called the mackey bowl. It felt slippery and smooth. I exclaimed, "Hey, this is so cool. It's silky smooth."

The big guy closest to me yelled, "Look, the new kid is running his hands over the mackey bowl and he likes it!" A chorus of "EWs" and "no fucking way" pounded my eardrums.

"Don't you know what a mackey is, boy?" asked a big guy as he spit loudly into the bowl. Twenty faces hooted at me as if I had just pooped my pants at the dinner table. I had no idea what a mackey was, and humiliated by my ignorance, I raced upstairs to our bedroom.

Frankie later explained it to me. A mackey is like spit, but not ordinary spit; a mackey is that yellow, gooey, oyster-like spit that boys, particularly farm boys, hack from the bottom of their throat and, at Spring Creek, expelled into the giant wash bowl in our basement. My embarrassment was overwhelming. One boy tried to nickname me "Mackey," but fortunately it did not stick—like the mackeys themselves. It was a lousy introduction to the farmhome.

Frankie told me that a few new boys got sent to the barn when Mrs. Weaver could not control them. So we hatched a daring plot to get me expelled from the house duties. My choice was keep dusting and die a slow death or risk it all. My brother spread the rumor that I was leading the other house boys to go on a work strike on Sundays. "Even the Lord rested on the Sabbath," was the battle cry. My Sabbath idea spread like wildfire, and Mrs. Weaver soon identified me as the ringleader. At the dinner table the very next night, Pop Weaver told me I was "too big for my britches" and would be on barn duty next week so he could keep an eye on me. "Wait till the big guys get you out behind the barn," he threatened.

I pretended to be chastened, but like Br'er Rabbit, the fabled trickster who succeeded by using his wits, I was secretly thrilled to be out from under the gloved index finger of Mrs. Weaver. As a barn guy I was closer to being a big guy, which was what I really wanted. But, I wondered, did they want me?

Life at a farmhome was rigorous. We spent our summer days weeding corn, baling and storing hay, painting fences, and bringing in wheat and barley. The bigger boys milked the cows twice a day, seven days a week, every week of the year. After the morning milking and house chores, we all sat down for breakfast. Growing boys who had already worked two hours and faced a long, full day of more physical labor, ate a lot. It was not uncommon for a barn guy to eat four or five eggs, six slices of toast, home fries, bacon or two thick slabs of scrapple, several glasses of milk and sometimes a bowl of cereal and never gain an ounce of fat.

Our cow barn was called a bank barn because its main floor where the milking took place was built into the side of a sloping bank. Because it was largely below ground, it provided some protection from the subfreezing winter temperatures in the Pennsylvania countryside. The cows did the rest. Their half-ton bodies were like massive furnaces fueled by wheat, oats, molasses, and corn silage twice a day. Those bovines kept the barn toasty on all but the bitterest of winter mornings. The milk house, a small attached building, adjoined the barn. The buckets of fresh milk went there to be strained into large milk cans. The cans were kept in a 35-degree water cooler until they were picked up for the Hershey Creamery.

My first day of what would be more than four thousand milkings began when I cautiously opened the big barn door and got my first close-up look at the cows. They were massive. As I marveled at these enormous creatures, number 208, bigger than a tractor, casually lifted her tail and took the biggest crap I had ever seen. I jumped back to escape the splatter of fresh, hot cow plop. The older barn boys had some laughs at my expense. One boy asked if I wanted to see the "star" on a cow's teat. I did. What ten-year-old boy would not want to see such a marvel?

He grabbed at the udders of number 208, and I moved cautiously forward.

"Can you see the star?" he asked.

"No, I can't," I replied.

He urged me closer and when I got about a foot away, he shot a stream of warm milk into my eyes and face that was so intense it knocked me back, and I narrowly missed the pile of fresh cow plop. The other boys howled in delight. I was busted.

My first cow was number 161. I got a bucket and milking stool. One of the big guys showed me how to grab the teat up close to the udder, squeeze and pull. I finally managed to get a few squirts of milk into the pail.

Then he told me I had to ask Pop Weaver for permission to start milking because I was the new kid. I did and was busted again. I annoyed Mr. Weaver by asking for permission that was not required. Moreover, in my brief absence from the side of number 161, she booted and flattened the milking stool, and the neighboring cow caved in the milk pail with her hooves. I was shocked by the casual power of the cows, and Pop Weaver was furious at me for destroying a good bucket and stool and getting the cows all riled up.

I managed to coax a half bucket of milk from number 161, a measly eleven pounds compared to the twenty pounds the cow normally produced. But I drew exhausted comfort in knowing I was on my way to being a real barn guy.

I was fully determined to pull my own weight and show no sign of weakness at any time. I raced to be the first to get to the barn in the pitch black mornings before dawn broke and struggled to shovel out the fresh manure that accumulated overnight in the gutter. But the physical demands of farm work on a ten-year-old boy were extreme. The first time I went baling hay on a hot August day, one of the senior bullies ordered me and another sixth grader to take up positions at the receiving end of the chute for the baler, which propelled fifty-pound bales of hay out to our hay wagon.

A huge bale of hay came down the chute and another was right behind it. I moved to the front of the wagon just in time to grab one of the two taut strands of baling twine that held the bale together. I strained with all my might and felt the twine cut into my hands. My flesh gave a bit, but the bale did not budge. The second bale came roaring down the chute and hit the first. My classmate strained as hard as I did and could not move the second bale. Then suddenly the third bale was pushing the first two bales and both of us toward the wagon's edge. The older boys howled with laughter at our plight. Tommy, one of the really cool seniors, arrived to rescue us and show us how to bale hay as a team. It took two of us to hoist a single bale of hay. By the third wagon, my hands began bleeding. Tommy, who was highly respected as a great athlete and leader, shocked me by loaning me his gloves. It was a rare act of kindness that taught me how much I wanted to be like him and not like the mean guys. A certain amount of teasing and kidding was part of the culture at the school. The bullies, however, routinely crossed a line into cruelty. Throughout my years at the school, I gravitated toward the boys, teachers, and coaches who were kind and thoughtful, and I aspired to follow their example.

The physical labor was not the hardest part of living at the farmhomes, however. Some of the bigger boys turned the younger boys into "slaves" forcing them to press clothes, shine shoes, and do other personal tasks. It was dehumanizing. My brother accepted the system as the way things were. I resisted it from the start as unfair. Tommy advised me to fight back at bullies just as the gruff meal-truck driver had. He told me that bullies were weak and sought out the boys who would fold easily. If you fought back, they backed off and looked for someone easier to pick on. It was a valuable lesson. One my brother would not heed.

One gray, cold November Saturday, we gathered in the barn for "whitewash day." It was the day when we cleaned all the crap off the walls of the barn milking floor and repainted them with a thick, pasty liquid called whitewash. It was a huge job and the house guys joined the barn guys to get it done in one day.

The worst part of the job was scraping off all the flecks of cow dung that had splattered on the wall when a cow coughed hard or sneezed in the middle of a huge cow plop. The excrement hardened like plaster. Shit-scraping detail went to the house guys and the little guys who worked in the barn. The big guys saved the best job for themselves: brushing on the whitewash.

I worked with Frankie who seemed nervous and uneasy and who complained that blisters were forming on his soft hands. He sought relief from Mr. Weaver who seemed to be in a hurry and waved him off. Two of the bullies took an interest in Frankie's complaint.

At break time for the noonday meal, we thought Frankie's transgression from the macho norm had been overlooked, but we relaxed too soon. One of our notorious bullies locked me in the milkhouse. By the time I got back to the barn, he and his accomplice had tossed Frankie into the big manure bucket that was used to carry cow dung. The manure bucket was attached to a track on the ceiling by a series of thick chains and pulleys. The tracks ran the length of the barn and out and around the big manure pit outside.

By the time I broke free, Frankie was jammed into a crap-lined iron box six feet off the ground that was now moving down the track. But before the bucket reached the manure pit where centrifugal force would fling it open, our substitute housefather appeared and stopped the show. Frankie hurt his shoulder, but most of the injury was to his dignity. One of my new buddies helped me clean him up, but incidents like that made him an even bigger target for the bullies.

Christmas was sadder than usual at Spring Creek because the Weavers made minimal effort to make the holiday festive. The sparsely decorated Christmas tree in the living room was not much taller than me. Some of the boys got to go home to visit relatives at Christmas. I vividly recall staring outside with Frankie and watching family visitors scoop up a few of our buddies in their loving arms as our tears turned to ice on the frozen window panes. Our new houseparents did not try to make the holiday brighter or easier for those of us left behind.

The quality of our lives was profoundly affected by the types of adults assigned to us. As with houseparents, we had great teachers and some not so great teachers. It was surprisingly easy to get on the wrong side of an adult who was predisposed to be angry, frustrated, or depressed. I became a target of my geography teacher on the very first day of sixth grade when my good friend Percy bounced a baseball glove off the back of my head in the hallway as we changed classes. The teacher demanded to know who threw the glove. We all just shrugged silently. Homeguys never betrayed one another. He seemed to know that I knew the identity of the culprit. From that moment on, I was squarely in his crosshairs.

I was so anxious to prove to him that I was trying to be a good student that I flipped over the cover page of our first geography quiz before he told us to start work.

He pounced: "Mr. O'Brien! Have I told you to start the quiz?"

He yelled so loud that his face turned as red as a ripe apple.

He ordered me to the front of the classroom, made me stand on a small twelve-inch-square floor tile, and told me not budge from the square while he struck me with a huge paddle ten times. After the tenth strike, I relaxed. He then struck again, for an eleventh time, and knocked me off the square.

"Too bad, boy. You just earned five more," he said. I swear drool dripped down his chin while he hit me five more times.

Outraged by his cruelty, I refused to show a bit of distress. And I felt an odd sense of satisfaction for having stood up to his unfairness. My classmates shared my grievance. Each one of us looked away from him in a mass display of disrespect.

He noticed. "You look at me when I talk to you!" he snapped.

We all stared at him like robots for the rest of the class and the rest of the week. We turned off our brains and tuned out everything he said. We refused to learn from him with a boycott of our minds. It was the only power we had. Just weeks later, he died suddenly of a heart attack. With the benefit of hindsight, I now realize that he was depressed and old and probably due for retirement. He was also experiencing domestic problems. Unfortunately for all, he took out his wordless grief on us.

I was terribly naive as a young HomeGuy and unaware that some of the boys at the school had deep emotional problems. One boy was nicknamed "Whacko"; we called him crazy to his face. Now I realize, he was indeed mentally ill. When Whacko first came to Spring Creek as a rising sixth grader, Pop Weaver found two kittens splattered on the concrete outside of our barn. When he looked up, another was hurtling down toward him from the top of a forty-foot silo. It had a barn handkerchief tied around its middle like a bandanna. Whacko said he was conducting a scientific experiment and building a parachute for cats to learn whether they do in fact always land on their feet. He engaged in other episodes of animal cruelty, a textbook sign of profound psychotic disorder in a child.

My brother displayed obsessive tendencies in those first years at Spring Creek. For instance, he was convinced he had spotted our Uncle

Ted's Chevy in town after Sunday services one week. He insisted we stake out that car every single Sunday, even after it became apparent that the Chevy almost certainly did not belong to our Uncle Ted. But he so wanted it to be "our relatives coming to rescue us" that he swore it was Ted's car. Frankie desperately wanted our grandmother to withdraw us from the school, and he wrote to her every single day for an entire year. He insisted I write the letter once a week, but it was mostly my brother's project. The letters rarely deviated.

Dear Grandma,

How are you? We are fine. We hope you are the same. We look forward to visiting you next summer.

But we don't think we can last that long. This is a scary, dangerous place. The older, big boys pick on us and make us their slaves. They make us do their ironing, shoe shining and other chores. They make fun of us and sometimes even beat us up.

The houseparents don't stop them and don't even seem to care about us. Not like the Arbogasts. The Weavers barely look at us except when they put us on detention. [Frankie later dropped this paragraph when he became convinced that school authorities were censoring our mail.]

So you got to take us out of here. We promise to be good and easy to take care of. We promise to pull our weight and not be a burden.

Please Grandma, come save us from this place. We can't take it anymore.

Love,
Frankie and Johnny

Our poor grandmother was devastated by those letters, but she was in no position to care for us, and she believed that a place that provided housing, food, and a good education was better than anything she could offer. She loved us enough to keep saying no and to keep sending us back to what Frankie called "our juvenile detention center."

At about that time, Frankie also began to conduct "research" into our parents and pressed our relatives in Snow Shoe for answers that they were reluctant to provide. He compiled a list of questions that the adults in our family steadfastly refused to answer. As we grew older, we realized our relatives were evasive on the subject of our parents. Frankie was convinced they had not died in a car accident, and he eventually learned that our father had been a wild boy who had been sent off to military school. After constant badgering, our maternal grandmother finally did show us a single photograph of our mother taken at her high-school graduation. We were dazzled into stone silence and spent hours just gazing at that image of our long-lost mother. It pained me when I could not recall a single memory of my mother holding or caring for me. Not a single memory of her at all. But I did sense a strong spiritual connection that I could not define. Frankie would sit with that photograph for hours during our annual summer week at our grandma's house.

I remember how unnatural it felt to return to the institution after even brief afternoons of freedom. After two whole weeks with our relatives in the summer, I always felt a sudden compulsion to flee or at least resist when the time came to return. I likened our plight to that of innocent boys being returned to jail after a short parole. Indeed, it was not so different. The institutional life of the orphanage shared more characteristics with a detention center than a regular boarding school. I always felt that we surrendered important chunks of ourselves to survive at Milton Hershey School.

At the same time, both Frankie and I took comfort in the familiar, the routine, the chores, and the same old faces. We swung back into Spartan life within minutes. It became Home because, practically speaking, it was all that we knew.

In those years, there was a Darwinian survival-of-the-fittest quality to the school. Those who thrived were tougher, luckier, and more resilient than those who did not. I thrived. I was blessed with brain power and an athletic ability that allowed me to rise through the ranks into a leadership position. But not every boy did that well. The boys who fell through the cracks haunted me for the rest of my life. Frankie was one of them.

5

FRANKIE'S STORY

Frankie (right) and Johnny arrive at the orphanage. *Provided by John O'Brien*

The boys like Frankie, who were pudgy, non-athletic and without the overt machismo of the typical HomeGuy, struggled at Milton Hershey School back in the 1950s. Even if they were smart, creative, and got good grades (like Frankie), they were subjected to merciless teasing and harassment. The bullies zeroed in on those kids like vultures circling carrion. It was as if they smelled the vulnerability. Frankie tried to make himself invisible, and he engaged in elaborate efforts to avoid gym class and recess by complaining he had headaches. He spent an inordinate amount of time hanging out with the school nurse during lunch period. When Frankie was still in the eighth grade, he sometimes hid during recess in a janitor's closet to avoid being bullied by the big goons. While the other boys exploded in unrestrained play during the brief midday break from the classroom, he cowered alone in the dark, closed space with his small Bible. The image of my brother seeking safety in that closet and some sort of solace in the scriptures still haunts me.

Mrs. Bickle, my homeroom and English teacher that year, was an extraordinary woman who made it her business to know and care about each of her precious boys. She was particularly kind to me and the other boys in my class who made a maximum effort. Mrs. Bickle knew how close I was to my brother and asked me one day how he was doing in high school. I started to blurt out the standard *everything is fine* line but then stopped and told her the truth, that he was being bullied by some big kids at lunch time. She told me to send Frankie to her husband, a high-school science teacher, who could always use another hand cleaning test tubes and equipment during recess. Frankie did visit Mr. Bickle's classroom, and even though he was not in any of Mr. Bickle's classes, he found the refuge and guardian he so desperately needed.

Mr. Bickle could only provide a brief respite, however. The more Frankie shrank from social engagement, the tougher it became for him. I tried to counsel my big brother and urged him to toughen up, go out for a sport, stand up for himself, and stand up to the bullies. But it was just not in him.

On the summer vacation before he began high school, we were in a car accident while visiting our relatives in Snow Shoe. Frankie, sitting in the front passenger seat, was thrown into the windshield when a young enlisted soldier, home on leave, ran a red light and plowed into our car. There were no seatbelts in those days. Frankie's forehead was covered by a spider web of fine scars that promptly got him the nickname "Frankenstein." Being heavy-set and awkward did not help. I have long wondered about that head injury. He complained about headaches and visual distortions after the accident. Did he sustain a traumatic brain injury that caused him to tip over the edge? In recent years, medical science has documented lasting and serious damage from traumatic brain injury for professional football players as well as for soldiers who are injured by improvised explosive devices (IEDs). We will never know.

I worried about Frankie, but being younger and desperate to fit in, I put me first. In my defense, I was struggling for survival and approval too, and I was just a little kid. So I was selective about when I went to his defense. I suspect I could not have done much more for him, but I regret not being able to save my brother to this day. The bullies kept piling on. After we returned from summer vacation the year Frankie was scheduled to start high school, two of the ruffians insisted he do all their personal ironing and shoe shining. When he refused, one put him in a headlock and forced him down on the bed and would not let him up until he agreed to do all his chores and apologize. I would have exploded in anger at such treatment when I was a ninth grader. Frankie apologized and enabled his tormentors even more.

At least our "institutional bubble" protected us from external threats. Most of the time, like many children in the United States, we felt threatened by the Communist Red Menace, the Cold War, and the Korean War. So we did the frequent "duck and cover" exercises required in most U.S. schools. When a classroom bell rang three times or Mr. Miller yelled "Duck and cover!" we dropped to the floor beneath our desk and rolled into a ball while covering our head. We shuddered until the all-clear sounded. Even at the time, we wondered how much safety a curled position under a flimsy desk provided in the midst of a nuclear attack. But no one skipped the exercises.

The news reels shown before the main feature at movies in town were terrifying. I remember grainy black-and-white images of airplanes dropping enormous bombs. Those shells floated down to blow away buildings, trains, and even people. The images formed the basis of a new nightmare. In it, I was on the Caaba playing-fields as the Koreans bombed us from Russian MiGs. In the movies, the bombs seemed to float forward as they fell, so in my dream, I ran as fast as my little legs would take me to the opposite end of the playground with those bombs in a slow but inevitable pursuit. I scampered until exhausted, and then I woke up in a sweat.

Frankie carried the Communist threat further than the rest of us.

In those early days of television, long before 24-hour broadcasting and cable, the handful of broadcast television stations put up a test pattern before and after their scheduled programming. The pattern in our area looked like an Erector Set windmill. We ignored the signal and just waited for our favorite shows: *The Lone Ranger* or *The Honeymooners*.

But Frankie became fascinated by the test pattern. One winter night, he shared his new secret with me. He swore me to secrecy and told me that he had detected a secret Russian code in the TV signal. I laughed and asked him if he had learned Russian. My deadly serious brother said no, but that the secret code was in symbols. He was convinced the Russian Communist bosses were communicating with Russian spies right there in Pennsylvania.

Later that week, I learned that Frankie had been caught staring at the TV signal in the living room in the middle of the night. It was a serious violation of the Milton Hershey Way. Every boy was supposed to be in his assigned, scheduled place at all times. Frankie was supposed to be in his bedroom and sleeping between 9 p.m. and 5 a.m., not sitting in the living room watching a test pattern on TV.

I worried less about the punishment he would get for being out of place than about what was happening to his mind. He had recently added the governor of Pennsylvania to his letter-writing campaign to get him rescued from the school. Mr. Bickle spoke to the principal, and they agreed to arrange for some counseling for Frankie. Getting psychological help at Milton Hershey School was risky business. The school had one part-time psychologist who seemed very nice, but no HomeGuy would ever admit to having any direct contact with her. It was the kiss of death to be seen near her office. The stigma was in proportion to ignorance of the causes and nature of mental illness. Those who had been sent to her were called "Whacko" or "Nutcase" and hounded unmercifully.

Frankie liked the psychologist. He said she really listened to him and was very smart. She asked him a lot of questions about the Russians. He thought she believed his story and agreed that the FBI was up to something. Within weeks, Frankie was being called "Psycho," even by kids he did not even know. He told me that his classmates were looking at him as if he was a freak in a carnival sideshow.

I felt bad for my brother, but I needed to survive in this jungle too. There were days in sixth and seventh grade when I felt I was "going under for the third time." I told Frankie he needed to act "normal," more like a real HomeGuy, and stop being so "gay." As soon as I said that word, I knew I had gone too far.

Homophobia was rampant at our all-boy school. Even being crazy was more acceptable than being homosexual. Nothing was worse. The American Psychiatric Association did not remove homosexuality from its list of mental disorders until 1973. Twenty years earlier, in the rural, closed world of Hershey and the even smaller world of the orphanage, homosexuality was one of the greatest taboos. I scrambled to take back the insult and told him I meant gay as in sissy, not gay as in homosexual. My brother was too wounded by my words to be mollified.

Later that week, he left the farmhome after bed check, hitchhiked into town and roamed around downtown Hershey for hours. That was an insane thing for a timid fourteen-year-old boy to do. Fortunately for my brother, a fair number of big guys sneaked out on a regular basis, and one of them spotted him and gave him a ride back to Spring Creek in his girlfriend's car.

Sneaking out, called "hooking out," was an art at the school. To be able to go over the wall at night, have some fun, and not get caught was greatly admired among the HomeGuys. If you were not an athlete or student leader, being a hook-out artist was your ticket to cool. The very idea terrified me. In fourteen years at the home, I never once hooked out, and my friends still tease me about being a wuss. I somehow understood that I was safe at Milton Hershey School, and I also wanted to please my favorite adults.

The key to a successful hook-out was to trick the housefather when he made his final round of bed checks each night. That meant making a dummy out of extra pillows and clothing to replicate the sleeping form of a teenager. The brightest delinquents forced little guys to sleep in their beds and made dummies for the little guy's bed because the housefathers never looked too closely there.

When word spread that Frankie had hooked out three times in two weeks, it boosted his reputation. For a few weeks, fewer kids called him "Psycho." Challenging the rules and authority was respected in our subculture.

His brief career as a hook-out artist marked the high point for Frankie. From that momentary pinnacle, life spiraled downward for my big brother. He couldn't get out for a fourth time because of the vigilance of our housefather, but instead would be found late at night in the furnace room or in the pantry. I followed him downstairs one night at 2 a.m. and asked him what he was doing.

He told me that he could see things more clearly at night. He explained that nighttime was when the truth emerged. He turned on the television to show me. When the TV test pattern came on, he excitedly pointed out a "change" from the week earlier.

"They changed the signal again!" he said too loudly for the late hour when everyone else was sound asleep.

"Who is they?" I asked.

"The Russians," replied my brother. "They are communicating with their spies."

That's when Pop Weaver popped in and caught us. I was less worried about the detentions than by what Frankie was doing. His fantasies scared me. And he kept saying he could see things "better" at night. As young and confused as I was, I sensed that Frankie was losing touch with reality.

During the day, he took to sleepwalking, literally. He would be asleep on his feet during morning chores, in his seat on the bus ride to school, and during some classes. When he started sleepwalking to lunch, some of the bullies nicknamed him "Zombie," another nickname made more apt by his lumbering gait. They made a contest and game out of who could wake him up.

Now I was really scared for my brother so I asked a high-school senior for advice. He suggested I get my brother transferred to another farmhome. To do that, I would have to ask the head of home life, Mr. Henry. Just making such a request was fraught with problems. I could only ask for a transfer if he agreed to keep the request in confidence. The Weavers would never let us live down an attempt to escape their control. To go to a school administrator by myself was as daunting as stopping by 1600 Pennsylvania Avenue and asking the president of the United States for a favor. It took me a couple of tries before I worked up enough courage to trail after Mr. Henry after lunch right into his office. He tried to brush me off and reminded me that students needed an appointment to speak with him. But I persisted.

I asked him if he could keep it just between us. Mr. Henry refused to make any promises. I had anticipated that he would not agree to my conditions, but my fears for my brother were so great that I blurted out that my brother was being badly bullied at Spring Creek and the Weavers did nothing to stop it.

Mr. Henry immediately defended the houseparents. He reminded me that Mr. Weaver was considered an excellent herdsman. I begged him for a transfer but I wasn't a very good beggar. He suggested counseling. I told him that Frankie was already seeing the counselor, and it only got him bullied more. He said he would think about it as he looked at his wrist watch. I walked away knowing that the likelihood of either a transfer or secrecy was poor.

In the following weeks, Frankie's behavior grew even stranger. The late-night strolls followed by the daytime zombie role continued. Then one Saturday, we were all working in the hay loft. Even the house guys were pulled into the chore of cleaning up the hay loft before the new summer hay would be put up. That meant pitching all the loose hay from broken bales down to the barn floor and restacking the unused bales so the old hay would not be covered by the new. Frankie was nowhere in sight, and I hoped he had found himself a secure hiding place.

Then I heard one of the more notorious bullies whoop that he had found "the Zombie's secret hiding place." Frankie was hiding in a little nest he had built out of hay in the loft. The tormentor started pushing bales of hay on top of Frankie and his little alfalfa fort, crushing him with the bulky bales. I was enraged. Without thinking, with all the love, frustration, and fear I felt for my brother, I raised my pitchfork and charged blindly at the bully. He heard me and jumped back to avoid the pitchfork tines coming toward his arm. Then he stumbled back another step and careened off the hayloft onto the barn floor. I heard the thud just seconds before hearing him scream about his arm being broken.

I was stunned. I had never before tried to intentionally hurt anyone, not even in barnyard football. I was numb. My mind went blank. I looked at the scene as if I was not even there, like I was floating outside of my body. My strong emotional reaction to my brother's plight shocked me.

Tommy, our student-home leader, told me that the "big guy" had it coming and promised to take care of it. I went to rescue Frankie who was still buried underneath bales of hay. He was all right, and it turned out that the bully only had a dislocated shoulder. But we still had to come up with a cover story. Tommy told Pop Weaver that the ruffian had gotten hurt in a pickup basketball game we hastily arranged. That was the final word. The HomeGuys would not deviate from the cover story. The injured boy would not betray me either. The code of silence would hold.

I heard nothing from Mr. Henry or anyone else about my request for a transfer. I became convinced help would never come, and then one day I noticed my brother was not on the bus after school. I asked around and discovered he had not been in his last afternoon class. One of his classmates said he thought my brother had been down to see the lady shrink. I worried all the way home. It wasn't like him to miss a class or the bus. When we pulled up to Spring Creek, I saw an official school vehicle parked there and hoped the psychologist had brought Frankie home from school.

I flung open the door hoping to see Frankie. What I saw was Mrs. Weaver talking to Mr. Henry, the head of student life, and the psychologist. Something was amiss.

My brother was not there.

I instantly knew something was wrong and blurted, "Where's Frankie? Is he OK?"

"Yes, he's OK," is what I remember them saying. "We need to talk about Frankie." They told me to sit down.

I sat on the very edge of my chair and looked anxiously into their eyes. The conversation went roughly like this. "You know Frankie has been having trouble adjusting to our Milton Hershey ways recently, and we have been trying to help him straighten out. Right?" Mr. Henry began.

I nodded, but I did not like the sound of "Milton Hershey ways" and "straighten out." My brother was not a bad or rebellious boy. Something was wrong with him, but he was no hoodlum.

The psychologist tried to explain. "Frankie's mind is playing tricks on him. He thinks people are out to get him. He is having great difficulty functioning in our institutional setting."

Mr. Henry explained further: "What she is trying to say is that it's not working here for Frankie. We're moving him to a special hospital."

I was confused. "Hospital?" I blurted. "He doesn't need no hospital. Is he sick or something?"

The psychologist tried to explain: "Yes, we think he may have a mental disorder and . . ."

Before she could go further, Mr. Henry interrupted. "He can't carry out the program. His chores, his studies, conforming to our behavior code. That is what this is about."

"That's why I asked for a transfer, Mr. Henry. He's being bullied. There *are* people out to get him!" I barked, raising my voice to authorities for perhaps the first time.

He then accused me of being "insolent" and said they were going out of their way to help my brother.

They told me Frankie was at the Philhaven Psychiatric Center. A school driver had taken him there that afternoon. I was both shocked and angry that they had not let us say goodbye to one another.

"He wouldn't leave without saying goodbye to me. Why didn't you let us say goodbye?" My shoulders hunched up to my ears and I could barely breathe I was so upset.

"Don't go flying off the handle now," warned Mr. Henry. I was too stunned to be flying off the handle. I didn't even have a handle.

The psychologist promised to take me to the center to visit Frankie that weekend. She said that it was only temporary, that he would get special help and then would come back.

Mr. Henry said Frankie should be back by the time we went on vacation, but he raised his eyebrows in a way that made me want to kill him. I somehow knew that these adults were lying to me and that my brother was not in a better place. The psychologist was nice, however, and I decided to hope for the best. I knew something was wrong with my brother. Maybe this special hospital could help him and make him better. In any case, he was better off being away from the hostile environment of the farmhome.

As the authorities left, Mrs. Weaver reminded me it was milking time. I could not believe that she was thinking about milking when my brother had been stolen away. It was almost like she read my mind, because she added that if I wasn't up for milking, I could help her in the kitchen. Kitchen? I might kill someone with a butcher knife if I stayed. Her suggestion got me up for milking, so I bolted, changed into barn clothes, and raced for the sanctuary of the barn.

Milking was one of my great escapes. For an hour or more, I could escape the adults, the rules, the supervision, the regimentation, the orders, and the pressure to fit in and be cool. I could just relax with my big gals and mindlessly harvest the product they wanted to be rid of and that the creamery in town wanted to buy. That night, I went far inside myself as I tried to figure out what was going on with my brother. I could almost milk in my sleep; all the big guys could, it had become an unconscious habit. I delivered one hundred pounds of milk that night to the milkroom strainer and had no recall of actually doing the chore. Some of my best thinking took place to the rhythmic whoosh, whoosh of the milk going into the metal pail when my head was buried into the side of a warm bovine.

I reflected. Frankie had been going downhill. Visiting the shrink hadn't helped. Had I done all I could? I was only twelve years old, but I had asked for a transfer and I had gone after the bully in the hayloft. I helped him get protection from the bullies at lunch through Mr. Bickle. Yet I felt guilty. I had stopped helping him with his letters and I left him alone each Sunday to stand by the Chevy he still insisted belonged to Uncle Ted. I ridiculed his stories about the TV signals and Russian spies. I felt I had abandoned my brother.

Now Frankie was gone. I would sleep alone that night. No goodnight chat or comforting hand hold. My heart dropped as I realized I had stopped holding his hand. I felt it was unmanly for us to be reaching for one another's hands at night as "wannabe big guys." We were too big for that. I felt so badly and wondered if he started hooking out because he thought I did not care about him any longer.

Nighttime pain penetrates more deeply than daytime anguish. Without the distractions of daily life, I dwelled on the plight of my brother and my worthiness and responsibility to him as his kid brother. Floundering in the misery, I suddenly realized that Milton Hershey School had a responsibility to my brother too. The school officials had done nothing to stop the frequent bullying. They ignored my request for a transfer. Why couldn't the school find more good houseparents who cared about the children and knew how to care for them? Even at that age, I understood that the school could have done more to save Frankie.

I prayed too. I was reasonably religious. Mr. Hershey was not a big churchgoer, but he was a Mennonite who drew upon the Golden Rule and the Ten Commandments for spiritual direction. The school required Bible readings in the student homes, some religious studies in the classroom, and mandatory worship service every Sunday. On that first night without Frankie, I prayed for Frankie's salvation as hard as I could. My prayer went something like this:

> Dear God, please protect my brother Frankie tonight. He is in a strange place with strange people and he is probably scared. Please be with him so he is not alone. Let him know that I have not abandoned him, that I love him and am coming soon. Please help him get better fast. Amen.

The following Sunday after worship service, the school psychologist picked me up and took me east toward Philhaven Hospital, a small, twenty-six-bed inpatient hospital founded by a group of Mennonites in 1952. During World War II, a group of young Mennonite conscientious objectors worked in state mental-health hospitals in lieu of military service. They decided there had to be a better way to provide mental-health services in their communities, and Philhaven was one of the small hospitals that resulted. At first glance, I was relieved. It did not look like a big scary hospital. It was made up of several one-story buildings, and the reception area felt like a homey living room. The reception staff and the nurse who took us to see Frankie were all friendly. But I was unsettled by the trip through the patient's wing. The hair on my arms and the back of my neck stood up at the sight of the doors to the patients' rooms. Each door was made of thick steel with a small window at adult eye level. They were all closed. Other than a few muffled voices and one shout, that could have been a scream, it was silent. We saw one other nurse, and no one else. It was secure, silent and empty. I remember thinking that it made Spring Creek seem like the *Howdy Doody Show*.

When the nurse opened the vault-like door, I saw Frankie sitting in a chair next to a hospital bed. As we entered, his eyes flickered slightly, but his expression did not change. My heart sank when he did not recognize me.

"Hey, Frankie!" I called out with gusto and a big, wide grin. A half-smile slowly crept up his face and his eyes opened slightly. He knew it was me.

He had not moved from the chair so I leaned over to give him a half hug.

"How're ya doin'?" I asked.

"OK," he replied in a weak voice. After a delay, he added, "Johnny."

Then he stammered out two questions: "What took you so long?" and "Where am I anyway?"

I felt some relief. This at least sounded like Frankie, and the questions made perfect sense.

Before I could answer, the nurse told me not to get him too "excited." Visits were limited to an hour. She pointed out the buzzer if we needed anything and then she left.

The school psychologist told Frankie he was at Philhaven hospital. "It's good to see you Frankie," she said.

Frankie squinted and nodded, but it was clear to me that he did not remember her and had no idea who she was. He had been at Philhaven for one week. "Hey, you're pretty," was all he said.

I told Frankie that I had wanted to come right away but the school would not let me and the hospital had said he wasn't ready for visitors. The psychologist stepped behind Frankie and shook her head in an emphatic "No."

"Whaddaya mean no? That's the truth. Can't we tell Frankie the truth?" She rolled her eyes and sighed. I was getting a little better at speaking my truth to authority.

Frankie asked for a Pepsi. In response to my questions, he said the people were nice, the food was not so great, and he had made a friend, Jody, who could see the secret coded messages the Russians were sending through the TV just like he could. Jody did not sound like a very helpful friend to me.

I asked him if he was well enough to come home.

"I dunno," mumbled Frankie, who suddenly looked exhausted, as if the few minutes of conversation had drained all the strength and energy from his body. He kept asking for a Pepsi.

He did not respond to my update on life at Milton Hershey School. Nothing seemed to be getting through, so I decided to find him a soda pop. The door was locked.

"What is this, a jail cell?" I barked at the psychologist.

"Calm down, Johnny. It is for his own protection," she said.

I impatiently and angrily pressed the buzzer, and a new nurse responded.

"Is something wrong?" she asked.

I was getting agitated. "We need to get him . . . We need to talk to the doctor. He can't stay," I stuttered.

The nurse advised me to slow down to avoid exciting the patient. Frankie hadn't responded one whit to anything.

I focused. "This is Frankie. He's my brother. Please don't call him 'the patient.' We need to talk to his doctor."

The psychologist added a "please" to my request.

The doctor did not work on weekends, and when I gave Frankie his pocket watch and quiz game, the nurse confiscated them, saying he was not allowed anything that might "over-stimulate" him.

Frankie looked like he could use some stimulation, but his old watch and a game to which he knew every answer were not about to make a bit of difference.

On our return trip to Hershey, I felt almost as depressed as Frankie looked. The psychologist explained that Frankie was on the latest *psycho*-something medication. It made him sleepy but would do wonders for his mind. I was confused by her diagnosis of *psychosis* and something-*phrenia*.

I just wanted him to come back home.

Despite the promise of frequent visits, I only saw Frankie once again before the scheduled vacation in July. The visit was a replay of the first, only Frankie was even more doped up than the first time.

Being without my brother was disorienting. I felt as though I were missing an arm or leg or even a head. Vacation at Snow Shoe was defined by his absence. The fact that we were more aware of his absence than we had ever been aware of his presence made me feel even guiltier.

When I returned after vacation, the psychologist was waiting for me in the foyer of the farmhome. I thought she might have good news about Frankie. Mrs. Weaver was talking to her.

"Hello John," said Mrs. Weaver. (She never did call me Johnny.) "We need to talk to you in the office."

I immediately began to worry. No good news had ever been delivered in the office.

The psychologist would not look me in the eye. That was not a good sign. She told me that Frankie had been transferred from Philhaven to Hollidaysburg State Hospital, a state mental asylum in Blair County. She said that the school thought it would be a better place for him. She seemed to have a hard time saying "better place."

Even in the 1950s, conditions in most state mental hospitals were deplorable. The mentally ill were warehoused for decades in facilities that were underfunded and understaffed. The staffers were often ill trained, if trained at all, and negligent. Some were just cruel and evil and exploited the mentally ill by preying on them, stealing from them, and treating them worse than animals. The large public mental hospitals were more like prisons than medical facilities. The use of restraints was common. Like medieval lunatic asylums, the hospitals were a way to hide the mentally ill rather than rehabilitate them.

Hollidaysburg State Hospital initially opened in 1904 as Blair County Hospital for Mental Diseases. The state of Pennsylvania assumed control in 1938. The facility eventually closed in 1979 as part of the nation-wide deinstitutionalization of the mentally ill. That historic movement scared the hell out of a lot of the communities the mentally ill were returning to, but mayhem never erupted. It did result in a rise in homeless and prison populations that is unchanged today.

Frankie, at the tender age of fourteen, was diagnosed with *schizophrenia*, a serious mental illness that typically is manifested by young men in their early twenties. It is unusual to find the disease in children. Schizophrenics suffer from delusions and paranoia, and they often hear voices. Social withdrawal and illogical thinking and disrupted sleep patterns are common. Frankie's symptoms were almost textbook. The causes of the disease are unclear. It could have been brought on by emotional trauma from our parents' death and worsened by the brain injury he suffered in the automobile accident. Studies conducted years later showed that children who experience severe trauma are three times more likely to develop schizophrenia. I will never know for sure if this is what happened to Frankie. But whatever the cause, Frankie was lost for good when transferred to the state's custodial care.

He was loaded up on what were the miracle drugs of the 1950s. Thorazine and lithium and, by 1954, chlorpromazine were used to treat the mentally ill. That is why he kept asking me for a Pepsi during that first visit. Dry mouth is a side effect of many psychotropic drugs.

Hollidaysburg State Hospital is near Altoona, Pennsylvania, about an hour from Snow Shoe. Our school psychologist suggested that our relatives could visit Frankie. I did the mental calculation and realized my brother was close to a four-hour drive from me and Milton Hershey School.

"I will never see Frankie again! Why did you send him further away?" I said heatedly.

The psychologist did not seem happy about the school's decision either. She kept repeating that the school felt it was a better place for Frankie.

I was developing an acute bullshit detector at the farmhome, and I sensed an opening.

"How could you turn your back on a good boy like Frankie? How could you?"

She nearly burst into tears and told me it was the "school's decision," hinting that she would have kept him at Philhaven longer.

Then her face and tone tightened and she said, "All school decisions are made in the best interests of the child."

It sounded like BS even to a twelve year old.

I immediately began begging for a visit, but the logistics at the time were daunting. Someone would have to take me on the four-hour drive. And the psychologist said Frankie would need to adjust to his new surroundings before anyone could visit him.

My confusion and shock over this decision outweighed my anger. That night I wrote Frankie a letter, and I wrote to him every night for the next ten days before receiving a response. I noticed his handwriting had gotten a lot worse. Frankie had won penmanship awards since the second grade. In his penciled note, the lines sagged and some words varied in size. I could read it, but my spirits sagged just like his scrawl.

He wrote a very brief note: barely two paragraphs. Every letter he wrote would start the same way: "Dear Johnny, How are you? I am fine? I hope you are the same."

"Fine?" And he hopes I am the same? His letter was contradictory. He wrote, "It's not too bad" and "I sleep a lot," but he also urged me to "come immediately" and "get me outta here."

The psychologist agreed to take me up on a Saturday but swore me to secrecy. No one at the school could know of our visit. Hollidaysburg State Hospital was a huge and old three-story brick building with black iron bars covering every single window. It looked like a prison. The visitor's room was a shabby, institutional room with thick glass walls separating state employees from the visitors. We sat on big, square, solid-wood chairs that looked as though they had been made in a Hershey Industrial School industrial arts class.

We were the only people in the visiting room, but a deep, husky voice shouted, "O'Brien! Visitors for O'Brien!" as if we were a football field away. An enormous man who looked more like an NFL lineman than a hospital aide said he would bring Frank in after we understood the visitor's rules. I immediately told him his name was Frankie, and the psychologist asked where Frankie's nurse was.

The bruiser's nametag identified him as "Leonard." He laughed at her question and said Frankie was lucky to have a bed, never mind a nurse.

I took a deep breath when someone who looked like my brother shuffled in on Leonard's arm. Frankie was slouched over, pale, and heavier, and he had a glassy-eyed stare. He did not recognize me until I called his name.

"Frankie, Frankie, over here." For the first time, I had to add, "It's your brother, Johnny."

He seemed spacey and disconnected. But when Leonard left the room, he perked up noticeably.

Frankie said I had to get him out of there because it was like a prison and said he wanted to go back to Philhaven. The fact that he wanted to go back to another psychiatric facility disturbed me. He said Hollidaysburg was a nuthouse and he wasn't a nut and the guards pushed the patients around and strapped them to their beds. One nurse threatened to shock him if he did not behave.

Leonard returned and my brother clammed up. When we asked if we could see the superintendent of the hospital, we were told we needed to make an appointment two weeks in advance.

We asked about sending presents to Frankie for the holidays, and before we left, Leonard handed us an index card on which he had written Frankie's purported clothing sizes: jacket, 48; shirt, X-large; pants, waist 46 and length 36.

Now Frankie was a big boy for fifteen, but Leonard was so stupid he thought we did not know my brother's clothing size. We quickly realized Leonard was writing down his own sizes because he routinely stole the gifts sent to patients in his care. I slept from emotional exhaustion for most of the ride back, and the psychologist promised to take me back to visit Frankie again at Thanksgiving. But it seemed the school had washed their hands of Frankie because they never took me to see him again or even spoke about him. It was as if he'd never been a

HomeGuy, as if he had never existed. Frankie was now the responsibility of his family and a ward of the state and no longer a concern of the school.

Eight months would pass before I would see Frankie again. My grandmother Carlson and Aunt June took me to see him during my summer vacation, before I was to start high school. He was getting fat, the result of medication and starchy institutional food. But he smiled when he saw us and recognized me and remembered my name this time. I watched the light in his blue eyes die as we said goodbye. On the way back to Snow Shoe, Grandma said she had given the hospital permission to try a new technique on Frankie. She did not tell me that it was electric shock therapy.

I knew Milton Hershey School had completely written off my brother when Mrs. Weaver announced that I had a new roommate. She removed all Frankie's personal items from the room. And poor Ridley, a pudgy, shy kid, moved in.

Frankie would never escape institutional custody. He would never drive a car, go on a date, or even take a stroll by himself. He would never choose a college or career, find an apartment, drink a beer, or decide what time to go to bed at night. My brother's dependency frightened me as deeply as it saddened me. Might I lose it all too? Frankie's lack of choice and absence of any control over his life taught me to cherish choice and to savor my freedom.

After I graduated from Milton Hershey School, I visited Frankie whenever I pleased. My brother had been stripped of freedom and dignity at the state hospital. Each visit followed the same pattern. As soon as a hospital guard ushered my brother into the visitor's room, I would hug Frankie and suggest we go outside for a smoke. I didn't smoke, but nicotine and candy were Frankie's drugs of choice, and I wanted to get him out of the hospital and that close, fetid air. I wanted to get me out of that institutional stench. My car was always loaded with his favorites. At each visit, he smoked a cigarette, ate a Hershey's Almond bar, smoked a cigarillo, ate at least two Reese's Peanut Butter Cups, and then said, "Can we go for a drive?"

I would always chide him to go slow as he gobbled down the candy and furiously smoked until I realized that this was the only freedom he might ever know. For two precious hours, he would be free of the oversight and regimentation of the hospital.

In the car, he would smoke again. We would go to a local diner for a cheeseburger, fries, a milkshake and a Pepsi, and then another cigar. At that point, Frankie would invariably throw it all up and ask me to take him home. That request always broke my heart.

By the time he was twenty years old, my brother was a broken man. The system had stupefied him. Home to him was now a state mental hospital.

During the national sweep of deinstitutionalization, Frankie's "cage" shut down like so many others across the country. I found him a bed in a nursing home about an hour north of Hershey. It was a nice, comfortable place in a rural setting. He liked it there. My brother could never live on his own. The shock treatment and the frequent use of restraints hastened his decline. What was probably worse for him was the degree of insanity among his fellow patients and some of the staff. The system itself was irrational and more than a little nuts. The institution with all its insanity became the new normal for him.

For several years, I dressed up as Santa Claus and brought gifts to Frankie and his pals at the nursing home. His entire face would light up like a Christmas tree when I came through the door. Frankie's bright blue eyes shining with childish delight are one of my favorite memories of my brother as an adult. My dear brother died at the age of fifty-five in 1997, a once-promising child who had been let down by a system that cared more about efficiency than his wellbeing.

6

FINISHING STRONG

Percy (right) and Johnny receiving Cocoa Bean Trophy. *Courtesy of the Milton Hershey School*

I am convinced that most children who lose their parents never fully recover from the loss. Losing parents at an early age leaves a bottomless well of yearning that cannot be filled. Of course, I recognize that children raised by loving relatives and adoptive parents may not feel the same way. But I was what they called "a lifer" at Milton Hershey

School, a child who arrived as a toddler and grew up there. Despite a rocky start, I was a well-adjusted boy by conventional measures. I studied hard, played hard, got along with my peers, and emerged as a student leader and star athlete in high school. I'd like to think my own parents would have been proud.

Yet nothing ever sated that core longing for love and acceptance in my tender youth. Some say I overcompensated. I was intensely competitive from the start. The nature of the competition was irrelevant. I wanted to win every spelling bee and every math contest, hit every baseball, and carry the football on every successful play. I was even willing to endure the "sissy chants" of my schoolmates to star in the elementary-school play—a female lead! I wanted to be first at the barn on those bone-chilling, dark mornings to milk the cows. I wanted to distinguish myself in any way I could because it showed the world that I mattered. I once lost in the final round of a regional spelling bee and was inconsolable. While I never understood why at the time, I pushed myself to be first in everything.

I was lucky that my natural abilities allowed me to excel academically and on the playing field. Sports also provided me with an acceptable outlet for the burning indignation that I usually managed to keep buried deep in my soul. It is not surprising that I became infatuated with football at an early age.

Pop Arbogast took me and the other youngsters at Caaba to my first football game one crisp autumn morning when I was eight years old. Our Spartans were playing York High School at Hershey Stadium. That day remains in my memory in brilliant Technicolor. The fall sky was a startling, crisp blue; the playing field was the greenest green I had ever seen; the very air snapped with excitement like clean sheets blowing on a clothes line in a gusty wind; Hershey Stadium was bigger than any building of my experience; and the intoxicating scent of chocolate wafting from the nearby chocolate factory permeated the stadium. My senses were overwhelmed. It was heaven on earth, and from the moment the Spartans ran onto the field in their brown-and-gold uniforms looking so big, proud, and fierce, I was hooked.

We each had a little brown-and-gold Spartan pennant, and we learned a cheer that we shouted at the top of our lungs.

> Brown and Gold! Brown and Gold!
> These are our colors. We are bold!

> Sis Boom Bah! Sis Boom Bah!
> Hershey Industrial—Rah Rah Rah!

That day was also the first time I set eyes on the steep hill that rose toward the clouds at the open end of Hershey Stadium. On the top of the hill was a building that looked like a castle. It was larger and lovelier than anything I had seen in a book, a true fairy castle worthy of a king. When Pop told me that it was Hershey Industrial School where the big guys attended class, my eyes and chest bulged out in wonder in what may have been my first swell of Spartan pride. Hershey is not a big place, but the isolation of our lives was so complete that it was possible to live for years in a Milton Hershey School cottage and never see some of the most compelling landmarks in town. The Spartans won that day, and all of us, including Pop, were euphoric. He let us chant a forbidden cheer on the bus ride back to our campus.

> Rooty Toot Toot! Rooty Toot Toot!
> We are the boys from the Institute.
> We don't smoke. We don't chew.
> We don't do what the other boys do.
> We want a lollipop—sucker!

The cheer never made a bit of sense to me, but we laughed and hooted ourselves silly every time we yelled the word "sucker" because it seemed so naughty. Watching our Spartans play football gave me a glimmer of belonging. I wanted to be on that playing field someday and do battle for the glory of my school. For the first time, I felt like I was part of something bigger than myself. I was not fully aware that something fundamental had changed, but hindsight helped me see that my brother and I had come to view Hershey Industrial School as Home. Even in grade school, we had spent more time at the school than any other place in our lives.

When Frankie went away for good, I was a teenager. After ten years living at the school, I had completely absorbed the ethos of the place. Milton Hershey School was my "normal." Part of me resented the authoritarian tendencies and regimentation, but I was a survivor, and like my fellow HomeGuys, I accepted and adjusted. Yet part of me also knew that someday I would go "over the wall" for good. And that promise of eventual freedom and perhaps the chance to rescue my brother from his prison kept me going.

Competition was intense for the limited slots on the school varsity and junior varsity athletic teams. The HomeGuys were no dummies. They understood that having a good excuse—glee club rehearsal, football practice, or band practice—would get them out of afternoon milking duty. About seven out of every ten boys tried out for some extracurricular activity. Those who did not make the cut got stuck milking the cows. But a miracle took place my freshman year of high school: the introduction of the milking machine.

The first milking machines to replace the tedious chore of hand milking were invented at the very end of the nineteenth century. They did not work well and were not popular with dairy farmers. Then Herbert McCornack invented the Surge Bucket Milker in 1922. It worked beautifully, actually harvesting more milk than human hands, and by 1955, the Surge Milker dominated 76 percent of the U.S. market. But change came slowly to Milton Hershey School, and the school also had a ready supply of free human-milkers, so we hand-milked until 1959. Although the Surge Milkers promised to free up our time, we initially resisted the change and acted as grumpy as the cows and Pop Weaver who regularly denounced the "newfangled nonsense." But once we adjusted, the machine cut the number of boy milkers in half. This meant more kids could engage in extracurricular activities and holiday vacations could last longer. As soon as we figured out the math, we loved those machines.

I was a little small, only 5 feet 4 inches tall and a lightweight at 138 pounds at the age of fourteen when I first tried out for junior varsity football, so the introduction of those machines may have made the difference between me making the team or not. If it weren't for those machines, the need for hand milkers might have kept a small athlete like me off the field and in the barn. In any case, I embraced football. Football changed my life and is one of the things that saved me.

Football, in many respects, is the quintessential macho sport. It is a primal collision of speed and power and bulk. It's no surprise then that boys of all ages are so drawn to the sport. I loved the game, particularly the hitting. To play football well, a player needs to give himself up completely and commit 100 percent to a collision, to a tackle, or to a block. Football allowed me the full expression and total release of my repressed spirit. I relished the pure, physical contact. Armored in all the protective gear, I could vent and lash out in an acceptable way. I felt alive.

I hit the books as hard as I hit the fullback from York High School. I still needed to be the best at everything. I studied so hard that my friends Percy and Carmen teased me about it. I used every free minute in preparation. When milking cows at 5:30 a.m., I studied German vocabulary and spelling with index cards I carried into the barn. With the electric milking machines, I got an extra ten minutes of focused study time with each Holstein. On the bus to school, I reviewed writing assignments and compared homework with my friend Terry, who was among the brightest kids at the school. I asked most of my teachers for permission to do a special project for extra credit. Some of my classmates resented my ambition, but my inexplicable need to achieve, win, and succeed drove me forward.

That drive is puzzling. I really had limited awareness of the world outside our Spartan bubble at that time. I still remember being awed into stunned silence at the beautiful sight of the Capitol Rotunda just eight miles away in Harrisburg, Pennsylvania, when I participated in a regional spelling bee. After correctly spelling words like "asymmetrical," "pulchritude," and "abattoir" (an easy one because we had an abattoir for butchering animals for food in Hershey), I made it into the final round. I thought I might win the regional bee and swaggered to the microphone for my final word. The word was "tyranny," a word I knew how to spell, but I heard something that sounded like "deerunhee." The word made no sense to me. I asked to hear the word the three legal times and still could not understand what word was being offered. I tried to sound it out and began with the letter *d*. The buzzer sounded and I jumped. When she spelled out "tyranny," t-y-r-a-n-n-y, my heart sank.

My all-time favorite English teacher, Mr. Hess, insisted we stay for the rest of the bee to honor the other contestants even though I desperately wanted to slink away in shame. I suffered through the remainder of that bee. On the short ride back to Hershey, I made excuses for myself about the sound system, the announcer, and the acoustics. Mr. Hess listened attentively and then asked me how I could have understood all the other words but not that last one? That astute question made me think.

Mr. Hess advised me to look inside, not outside for the answer to my failure. He helped me understand that I was listening for a hard word, not a word I had known since fifth grade. "Might you have been temporarily hard of hearing?" he asked with a grin. I eventually came to see that I was trying too hard and was too intense, and that intensity and ambition got in the way of my ability to perform. I was to relearn that lesson many times, and even today I am forced to think of Mr. Hess's wise advice to be calm, open, and present.

This was among the many lessons that I took from those years. My experiences as a teenager at Milton Hershey School formed my character as an adult and informed my tenure as the school's leader many years later. I had a lot to learn. Despite my small size, I burned to be a varsity player and show I had the right stuff to be a first-string Spartan. During my sophomore year, we played an away baseball game in Harrisburg when I was summoned from the bench to replace our catcher, a senior who went down in a home-plate collision. I felt pretty confident. The pitcher only threw fast balls and was fairly easy to catch. All went well until the fifth inning. The batter squared off to bunt as our pitcher threw a fastball right down the middle. Unfortunately, the batter ticked the top of the baseball just enough to deflect it slightly downward and straight into my crotch at full speed.

Somehow, I had never learned that catchers routinely wear a hard, molded, plastic cup in their jock-straps to absorb such brutal assaults. Is that something a parent or coach might tell their boy? I went down like a rock and writhed in an agony beyond belief. Then I remembered our football coach Bob Klingler had taught us the proper response to a shot in the groin. "Okay, you guys," he instructed, "if you get hit in the balls, grab your head. You don't want to grab your crotch and make a painful situation even more embarrassing." We all snickered and took our own shots at each other's groin, but the strange advice stuck with me.

So against all instincts, I grabbed my head. I groaned and groveled in the dust at home plate with my hands firmly locked onto my temples. The umpire asked, "Are you okay, son?" I could barely grunt in response. Coach Rather and our student trainer finally arrived and coach asked what was wrong with my head.

Head? Didn't he know the secret code for crotch trauma? Furthermore, hadn't he watched the flight of the last pitch? I grunted to no avail. Then I grunted and looked down at my groin.

"I don't think it's his head, sir," Stevie, the student manager said. "I think it's his private parts."

Ungh. Ungh! I grunted twice in confirmation.

"Oh yeah, you're probably right. Weren't you wearing a cup, Johnny?"

What cup? I'd never heard anything about a cup! And how did that matter now? I needed relief, not a lecture.

"Okay, I've seen this before," Coach Rather said, and he grabbed me underneath both of my armpits and started dragging me around home plate. Apparently, some of the students and fans of John Harris High School had also figured out my predicament and I heard a "Go-nad!" chant start up along with some female laughter. I thought I knew the depths of embarrassment, but I had never before suffered humiliation—so public and total—like this. Moments ago, I was a studly Spartan catcher making his first varsity start. Now I was a crumpled sophomore, whose fragile manhood had been compromised, being dragged around the batter's box until dirt obliterated the proud Spartan logo across my jersey.

Wounded, I eventually ended up back at the farmhome in bed where I was in such agonizing pain I remained still even after the 5:15 a.m. bell sounded. Suddenly, the hallway light was blotted out.

"Why aren't you gettin' yourself out to the barn, Johnny?" Pop Weaver asked, implying that I had already done something wrong.

"I—uh—got injured at the baseball game yesterday, sir," I replied, knowing that he already knew that.

"Can't milk? Can't go to school today! Can't go to practice!" he squeezed the vise.

I hobbled to my feet while dropping my pajamas, hoping that he might see the sorry state of my family jewels and cut me some slack. My housefather looked and he saw the purple eggplants bulging four feet away, but he chose to cock his head and say, "You'll be late for the barn in ten minutes!"

"Hey dumbass! Get back in bed," my friend Pluto hollered when he saw me shuffling down the hallway.

"What and be stuck here all day by myself with these imbeciles?" I answered. He grinned and grimaced at the same time.

With help, I made it to the barn just in time, and several of the big guys rotated in my direction to do all the heavy lifting for me. Home-

Guys were particularly tight that way. We could be fighting or ignoring one another one moment and pitching in to help a brother in real trouble the very next day—especially if it helped him beat the system.

I finally made the varsity football team in my sophomore year, but being among the youngest members of the team, I sat on the bench and watched more than I played. The year 1959 was supposed to be a banner year for the Spartans. The team had some incredibly talented senior players, and local sports writers pegged Milton Hershey School as one of the best teams in the area. The regimentation of the orphanage was fantastic training for young athletes. We ate three square meals a day of healthy food and rarely ate junk food. We got lots of rigorous exercise doing farm work that built out our young bodies into highly muscled machines. Smoking was forbidden, although some boys snuck cigarettes. And we got eight hours of sleep—from 9 p.m. until 5 a.m.— every single night. In some respects, we were in permanent physical training.

The year 1959 was also the fiftieth anniversary of the founding of the school so expectations for a banner year were high. Despite the big build-up, however, the football team folded and fell behind in game after game. Having a lot of bench time to observe, I finally realized the team lacked leadership. Instead of working together, the best players competed against one another to get the ball to improve their individual stats. There was little team work; most of the players were out for themselves. I had always taken team spirit for granted, but after watching this meltdown, I realized a team needed leaders and team players to be effective. I vowed to be both someday.

HomeGuys lived by a code of absolute loyalty to one another, even the boys who were outlaws and bullies. It was our own version of the Mafia's omerta, a code of silence and honor that bound us to one another and against the authorities. One day a senior defied the smoking ban on our bus and got into a fist fight with the bus driver. He not only bested the driver and threw him out the door, he hijacked the bus and drove it all the way to Old Senior Hall! That student, Louie, was expelled from school just three weeks before graduation. We were awed by his audacity and excited by his dramatic insubordination. We hooted and hollered as Louie drove the bus all the way to Old Senior Hall, where we got deathly quiet when the authorities arrived to put down our fifteen-minute rebellion.

Nothing thrilled us more than rebellion against authority. We wanted to lash out against the system and take back a modicum of self-respect from the stifling institutionalization of the Home. The system did not allow for much individuality or original thought, so we became a lot like our cows. We often felt like docile automatons moving in a herd. And dairy farming actually took precedence in many respects over child rearing. Yet something kept me sane and steady and focused. I am not sure what. And every day, I swore to myself that I would become someone who mattered. During the disastrous 1959 football season, my friends and I decided when our turn came to be the starters on the team, we would boast less, work as a team more, and get in better shape than any of our opponents.

John F. Kennedy won the presidential election of 1960, my junior year of high school. Like so many young people, I was dazzled by the handsome, charismatic Massachusetts Democrat. He seemed so clear, focused, and decisive in the presidential debates we watched on television. I wanted to be like that; I wanted to be a leader. Mr. Hess, my wonderful English teacher, recommended I read Kennedy's book *Profiles in Courage*, a series of profiles on leadership that won the Pulitzer Prize in 1957. I became president of my junior and senior classes and led my class in academic standing. I grew about five inches and gained forty pounds in my first two years of high school. The hay baling, milking, and shoveling chores of farmhome life hardened my body for the contact sports I craved so I also became an important member of the varsity teams.

I learned another lesson when I was a high-school junior: the importance of serendipity and luck in life. During a pre-season scrimmage the August before my junior year, I took down our team captain and starting quarterback in a routine tackle that broke his right forearm. Harry was our respected leader, and I was horrified by the accident. Although I did not feel ready for the challenge, I became the starting quarterback a good year earlier than I dreamed.

Coach Klingler, a fabulous life mentor as well as athletic coach, took me to the school infirmary to see Harry after the accident. The coach made me understand that the injury was not my fault. "Football is a violent sport. You made a perfect form tackle," he reminded me. Harry was a good sport about it and joked that he knew I would take his job someday but didn't realize it would be so soon. I can't imagine taking a career-ending injury so pleasantly. His laughter and kind words relieved my conscience like helium whooshing from a balloon.

That season was a rude introduction to leadership for me. We lost every single game that year, the first athletic team to do so in recent Milton Hershey School history. But even though we did not win our games, we kept getting better. While I did not suddenly emerge as an effective leader, that experience represented a crucial introduction to the importance of self-confidence, conviction, and persistence.

I continued to ace all my classes. In the Milton Hershey School grading system, an A, the top grade, was a 1. I wanted a 1 in every subject and got it. Every once in a while, I got a 2, but it was for conduct, not academic achievement. I was a teenager, after all, and the rules and authority made me bristle and inspired me to creatively game the system. My buddies and I rarely got caught, but when we did, a 2 or 3 for conduct showed up on my report card.

Becoming an official "big guy," as an upper classman, only made me more focused—almost obsessed—to succeed. During the summer break at Snow Shoe before my senior year, I ran a six-mile loop around town in the dark, defying barking dogs, potholes, and glimpses of shot-guns every single morning. Few people jogged intentionally in the late 1950s. After Grandma's substantial breakfast, I did calisthenics and used the single dumbbell my uncle Leroy owned. I tossed a football in the backyard to Leroy when we had a break from chores. Back at the farmhome, I tossed a tight spiral over and over again between an old truck tire hung between two large tree limbs. I had joined Glee Club, and I practiced singing in the outhouse and while I jogged. The spiders and mice in the old outhouse did not seem to mind at all.

After losing every single football game during our junior year, the team was primed for revenge. All that loss, all those setbacks had taught us to work as a selfless, seamless unit. In our first game against Hershey High, the famed Cocoa Bean Bowl, we won 25-0. It was our first victory over Hershey High in four years and our first football team victory in fourteen months. Something flipped in my heart as I ran the second-half kickoff back for a touchdown in the pouring rain. Our soaked, muddied, and exhausted orphan army was as thrilled as any band of teenagers in America that Friday night.

By winning the Cocoa Bean game and then scoring a big upset in the Homecoming game, we already had a pretty good season. But we also suffered several heartbreaking losses to central Pennsylvania "giant schools" and had to face the best of the gargantuans in our final two games. Cedar Cliff High School was 8-0 and favored over us by four touchdowns by regional sportswriters. Then we would finish at Lancaster McCaskey High School, who had just racked up their nineteenth straight win and were ranked number one in most state polls.

Cedar Cliff was the last home game for us seniors who had endured so much adversity together. We were not just teammates; we were brothers. And we had developed a deep and quiet pride that reflected my friend Percy's leadership style: giving everything he had all the time and expecting us to do the same. I was the good cop. If Percy got in your face for lack of effort, it was a moist and scary experience. We all lifted our game that day because we knew Percy would and that he'd be watching. That made us dangerous.

We took the field at Hershey Stadium for the last time on a beautiful Saturday afternoon to our Spartan Band's blaring rendition of Chuck Berry's "Johnny B. Goode." Back then I was so self-absorbed that I took the instruction literally. Even the sight of a huge visitor's crowd, "gathering for the slaughter," didn't faze us. Our coaches had prepared us for that huge, noisy crowd, and we had seen so many before. "Our family is right here in this locker room!" Coach Klingler hollered.

"Look around. Remember what we've been through together. Brothers—not teammates," I implored. Percy just hissed, "Let's go shock 'em!" My cleats barely touched the turf during warm-ups.

Everything started to open up when Gordy scored on a slant pass I threw his way. Carmen led our running attack and slammed in for a second score. Our hoppin' mad, swarming defense shut everything down, and then Percy shocked 'em alright with a dazzling punt return that left Cedar Cliff tacklers strewn everywhere. I got a TD after a long drive, and Terry Henry, our sawed-off sophomore southpaw, completed the scoring on a reverse pass to my roommate Steve Russell. Milton Hershey School: 37, Cedar Cliff: 7. Shock and rout.

We strode as tall as Wilt Chamberlain on our farewell trot out of Hershey Stadium. Yet we were stunned by the totality of our conquest. Coach Klingler picked up on our bewilderment and made sure to dispel any doubt. "This was no fluke," he assured us in the post-game delirium. "This is what we're capable of boys. This is what we're taking on the road to Lancaster!"

We hooted, hugged, and howled all the way to Old Senior Hall where we became ordinary, proud HomeGuys headed to our respective farms, praying that we were too late for the evening milking.

"This assignment is more important than a mere sports contest," Mr. Hess pointed out when I asked if I could get an extension on a term paper that fateful week. Then he winked and said, "But I'll take a draft by the due date." That was his way of cutting me a little slack while not showing outright favoritism. But when I asked "Mr. A," the director of Glee Club, for permission to miss a rehearsal that week, he said, "Who do you think you are Mr. Quarterback?" Few athletes ever joined our renowned Glee Club, but I found it to be fun and even better than sports for getting excused from evening milkings. As for the "sissy thing," heck, I had already starred as a girl in two elementary-school plays.

I didn't want special favors, and I knew slack wasn't forthcoming from my houseparents. It puzzled me that the more success I had, or my roommate Steve had, the more resentment we felt. We thought our achievements would reflect positively on Spring Creek and the Weavers, but it seemed to earn us more work. The last time I'd heard a word of encouragement or praise from a houseparent had been from Pop Arbogast in the fifth grade.

Old Senior Hall was jazzed that fateful November week. It focused more on our remarkable thrashing of Cedar Cliff than our having any chance against Lancaster. Maybe Spartan country was influenced by the local sportswriters, who were favoring Lancaster by an unheard-of five-touchdown margin. I'm not sure any of us believed we had a chance of knocking off mighty Lancaster as we completed our very last practice together and trotted to the locker room. I know I didn't. But something visceral was in play, and Percy, who rarely made remarks to the entire team, got up and the locker room got study-hall quiet. "They expect us to roll over. Anyone planning to roll over? Shit, we'll die before we ever roll over. Hell, let's take our ragtag orphan army down to Lancaster and roll right the fuck over them!" The place went nuts. No one but Coach Klingler heard Percy's "Excuse my language" above a din that matched the psych ward at Hollidaysburg Hospital. There was no following that act and I didn't try.

As mentally ready as we were to confront a huge and hostile crowd, tremors competed with goosebumps as we filed off the school bus, donned our shoulder pads, and literally pushed our way through the throngs of Lancaster fans to get into their stadium. These were some dedicated fans. They didn't seem to notice or care that the enemy had entered their sanctuary. I glanced up at what looked like a Rockwell "Thanksgiving" family portrait and felt a huge stab of envy. Families held signs imploring their precious sons to triumph today. How great would it be to play for a real family? Amazingly, I would not notice the crowd again until the final whistle blew.

It was the rarest of afternoons when I thoroughly lost myself in the game. Everything—the fans, the stadium, an opponent's size—evaporated. All I did was run, throw, tackle, and get tackled very hard. Nothing else mattered. Carm, Percy, Tony, Tom, and most of the Spartans on the field played the same way. Time seemed to slow down. I had never seen the field so clearly before, a visual acuity allowing me to see order in the chaos and sharpening every facet of the game. The other surprising gift was the constantly renewed energy all of us felt. The harder we played, the more energized we felt. There was something about performing together at peak levels that enhanced our clarity and refueled us.

We trotted off the field at halftime pleased but surprised at our 6-0 lead. No one had held Lancaster scoreless in the first half in years. While I had scored on a short touchdown run, Percy had set it up with two twenty-yard bursts. I was still berating myself for not kicking the extra point through the uprights.

A hush grew over our halftime locker room as we sensed it was time. The biggest thirty minutes of our young lives. "It's time. It's our time, boys," Coach Buser intoned. "Your victory here today will be the best memory of your lifetime."

"We're special, you know," Coach Klingler half-whispered, so we had to lean in to hear him. "This team, our family, you boys are special, but out there they treat us like we don't even exist. Let's go out and show 'em that we're special." Coach surely knew that each one of us would die to feel special. We rose in unison and stormed out on the battlefield.

Every time Lancaster got inside our forty-yard line. Percy, Tony, and half the team would rise up and stop them. We clung to a precarious 6-0 lead and our opponents, knowing they were in a rabid dogfight, stiffened their defenses. Late in the third quarter, Lancaster blocked our punt and scored a few plays later. Their kicker did make the extra point. Lancaster 7, Milton Hershey School 6. The Lancaster fans went wild. They were boisterous the first quarter, stunned quiet in the second by our score, and delirious now.

On this day, the underdogs were not backing down. After an exchange of punts, we finally moved the ball all the way down to the two-yard line after Carm caught my pass for a critical thirty-six yard gain. Fourth and goal from the two. Our season, our athletic career, and our very HomeGuy souls were on the line. No one was thinking field goal. We, well I, had trouble making extra points. No, we had come too far together to settle for anything less than a touchdown.

On this drive, Tom, our All-State center, had already knocked down two defenders to allow me to gain eleven yards on a quarterback sneak. Guess what play we called? But this time, there was nothing sneaky about it. Lancaster was ready for the play as I stayed low and hard on Tom's substantial buttocks. Whomp! Bam! Bodies were piling up at the point where there should have been a little daylight. Tom kept his legs churning and so did I. With one last lunge to the left, I collapsed under what felt like a dozen players and a faint, muzzled whistle blew.

"Touchdown!" the referee yelled and at least ten Spartans whooped in unison. I was just too relieved to whoop when I saw the ball just barely in the friggin' endzone. Milton Hershey School 12, Lancaster 7. Yes, I had missed another kick!

With HomeGuys gang-tackling their asses off, we held the state champions at bay. With only three minutes to go, I thought, "The clock is our friend." But time slowed as Lancaster mounted a punishing drive. Their All-American Ken Stoudt's phenomenal speed finally got him past our secondary for a forty-yard bomb. With just under a minute to go, the Red Tornadoes reached our five-yard line. But a Lancaster penalty nullified what appeared to be a touchdown. We went from agony to hope in seconds. It was still only third down, and a half minute remained.

Pandemonium filled Red Rose Stadium. Every spectator believed the Red Tornadoes would punch the ball in and restore sanity. I had a sinking feeling myself. Until I looked at Percy. He seemed to be smiling and drooling simultaneously. We looked around the defensive huddle for what we knew would be the last time. Tool, Steve, Ed, Tom, Chuck, Tony, Percy, and Carm—our band of brothers had lined up to defend

Spartan turf for practically every play in the last two years. We were covered in dirt and blood.

No one spoke. We just nodded to one another. Lips pursed, jaws set, eyes riveted, we moved our heads up and down just enough to confirm we were making our very last stand. The Red Tornadoes broke their huddle in pure silence and so did we. If there was stadium noise, as there surely was, I didn't hear it. All we heard was the quarterback cadence. Then all hell broke loose.

It was a pass play and I moved quickly to help Percy cover Stoudt across the middle. Percy wasn't there. He had decided on his own to blitz and attack the quarterback. The sight of Percy completely vaulting over the blocking fullback to land a smothering blow on the quarterback's head was one of the most remarkable feats I've ever witnessed. Now third and sixteen with a few seconds left. More angst, but on our final play as Spartans, our gritty line that had played ferociously all day forced the quarterback to throw wide.

Silence. Then our unbridled screams of pure joy joined the sound of "Onward Spartans" from a stunned but delirious Spartan Band. Our bench cleared and our few, loyal Spartan fans made their way to the endzone we had successfully defended. Now a quiet pile of joy. No loud cheers—we were too tired and shocked. Proudly we hugged. As athletes, especially clad in our armor, HomeGuys hugging HomeGuys was okay. Permission would not have been necessary on that November 12 afternoon. I hugged everybody within reach—even some elderly woman I had never met.

All embraces with my teammates—my brothers—were special. We had sacrificed and come so far together. Some were sacred—the embrace that Percy, Carm, Tony, and I shared under the goalposts that were being torn down. A heavy slap on my shoulder pads got me to turn around to a "Hey champ—we did it"; and the warm embrace I shared with a moist-eyed Coach Klingler was the second-best adult hug I'd ever remember.

Head Coach Buser put one arm around me and said, "You made us all very proud, son." I fought back tears. It was hard to get very close to Coach Buser, but I respected him to the core.

By beating the number-one-ranked team in the state on their field, we made history. Some sports enthusiasts would say it was the biggest high-school upset of the decade, and certainly it was the most important victory in the Milton Hershey School record book. As with most athletes, what mattered was the fact of being in the battle, giving all we had side-by-side with people we cared deeply about. The headlines, the accolades, and the attention were sweeteners, like cake icing. Being there—being totally, unconditionally there—in a great cause larger than ourselves, there's the magic.

How we got out of the stadium and onto the Spartan school bus and back to Hershey is still a mystery to me. I vaguely remember our determined orphan army of fans bringing down one of the goal posts and irate Lancaster boosters pelting our band bus with stuff. It wasn't until a week later when a seasoned alumnus gave me a section of goal post engraved "Milton Hershey School 12—Lancaster 7" that I was sure it actually happened.

What I remember about the return trip was being naturally high and unnaturally happy. And proud. Spartan proud. To think that our little high school that hadn't won one game last year could defeat the mightiest warriors in the great football state of Pennsylvania. How could that have happened? How could sixty minutes of anything turn throwaway teenagers from insecure doubters to confident conquerors—especially in a way that endured? The Lancaster victory injected a measure of grounded confidence in the entire student body for the rest of our senior year. Well beyond that, most would say.

Some years would pass before I would understand that my high-school football career was not about football. With enough daylight and a little maturity, I grew to see it as a profound tutorial on life. The star-studded, underachieving team of my sophomore year was a classic study on the pitfalls of pride, ego, and self-centeredness. Our winless junior year was a textbook on the pain and potential promise of massive adversity. It taught us that adversity—if well-processed and mined for wisdom—can become an enormous advantage. And then, from our magical senior season, I learned the unlimited possibilities that exist when people unselfishly unite to give all that they have in a common cause.

We have all read those truths in countless bestsellers on human potential. But I needed to experience them viscerally and repeatedly, and then I had to process the meaning to fully internalize their brilliance. Maybe we all do.

After our phenomenal football season, I continued to focus like a laser on being successful. I wanted to be the valedictorian of my class and gain admission to a college like Slippery Rock, the state school known for teacher training; or Gettysburg, a local private school; or maybe even Penn State if I got lucky. But that final football season attracted useful attention. Football got me named to the Pennsylvania All-State Team, the top thirty-three players in the state as compiled by the sports writers. The awards snowballed: the B'nai B'rith Foundation named me "Sportsman of the Year" for Central Pennsylvania; I was named winner of the Thom McAn Trophy as "High School Player of the Year" for Pennsylvania. Part of me fretted over the accolades because it shorted the contribution made by my friends and teammates like Percy, Carmen, Gordy, and Tom. And there was no way in my mind that I was the best player in the state. Heck, I did not even think I was the best player on our team. And by the way, there was a quarterback from Beaver Falls named Joe Namath and a fullback from Scranton named Cosmo Iacavazzi who were pretty darn good!

It was shocking how I found out about the High School Player of the Year award. Having won a free subscription to the local newspaper by being a finalist in the regional spelling bee (yes, that disaster), I discovered I had won the award by reading the newspaper one Sunday morning. Pictures of me and the trophy were featured in the lead story. I was stunned. No one at the school had bothered to mention it to me. I wondered briefly what real parents would do if their sixteen year old were honored in that way. My feeling of awe quickly displaced any disappointment at the lack of attention from Milton Hershey School officials.

In December, I returned to my farmhome for evening milking and found a dozen recruitment letters from colleges. Some of the letters were two or three weeks old. I guess the school had "protected" me from this information as well. The schools included Notre Dame, Cornell, Army, Harvard, Navy, Princeton, Penn State, and Pitt. I was dumbfounded.

Sidelined by a torn tendon incurred during the Lancaster miracle, I had time to consider colleges because my injury made it impossible for me to play basketball that winter. But that meant a return to the dreaded evening milkings! Even so, much to everyone's surprise, Milton Hershey School allowed me four college trips. The school thought that uniformity was the key to peace and prided itself on not allowing any boy extra privileges. Little coaching would be forthcoming from my alma mater. The school did not have a college counselor because only about one-third of our seniors went to college, and most of them went to Hershey Junior College in town for free.

What a big decision for a boy who had so little practice making them! I wanted a school that was personal, with warmth and personality. I did not want to be on a big impersonal campus. I also wanted to go to a college with a first-rate academic program. Being largely confined to the Milton Hershey School bubble, I had never heard of the Ivy League, so I quickly asked my faculty mentors. When I made the first cut, I settled on Army, Cornell, Navy, Harvard, and Princeton. I had gotten an appointment to the Naval Academy, but that got nixed early when they learned my vision was well below the required 20/40 without correction.

My first visit to West Point was also my first trip out of state, first train trip, first stay in a hotel, first cab ride, and first trip without adult supervision. The regimentation and discipline of West Point resonated with me; I had lived in that type of environment for my entire life. But I was repelled by the hazing that was considered an essential Army tradition. It sounded too much like the bullying system at Milton Hershey School. I felt I needed a structured college environment like West Point, but something else was bothering me. My host, a cadet who was also a quarterback, pulled me aside to tell me that West Point was not a place to go if I wanted to enjoy college and savor freedom. My subconscious was telling me that I might just be substituting one institutional home for another. His whispered confidence prompted an epiphany. I desperately wanted to be free, but I also feared that freedom. The fear of freedom felt almost paralyzing at times and threatened my dying thirst for independence.

So I reluctantly crossed West Point off the list. Then I took my first airplane ride to visit Harvard, where I found Boston overwhelming and a little bit scary. And I had my first martini by mistake on the Cornell visit—a mistake that caused some memorable and embarrassing intestinal challenges. But I was beginning to hone in on the qualities that I wanted in a school. My final visit was to Princeton. I knew I was being wooed, but there was something special about the coaches and their warmth and genuine interest in me. I was floored when Coach Colman quietly advised me to go to Cornell or Harvard rather than a big football school if I decided against Princeton. He told me to put my education first. And Coach Jake McCandless treated me as I imagined a real father might. Princeton seemed pretty inviting.

My three final choices, Harvard, Cornell, and Princeton, accepted me for admission. The next challenge would be how to pay for college. The three Ivies would cost up to $5,000 a year: not much today, but a fortune to an orphan who would leave Milton Hershey with nothing but $100 and a small suitcase of clothing.

The three colleges not only accepted me but offered substantial scholarships. With my campus job, summer job, and loans factored in, I would have enough to cover everything. It was more than I ever could have dreamed.

But how to decide? I received congratulatory phone calls from Harvard and Cornell within twenty-four hours, and as Saturday afternoon drifted toward evening milking time, I wondered why I had not heard from Princeton. Harvard, for all its glory and prestige, didn't feel right to me. The big city and its sophistication were just too alien. My German teacher had taught me to write down columns of good points and bad when it was time to make a big decision in order to make an objective assessment. Cornell and Princeton both scored high and evenly.

I was leaning toward Princeton as I went out to the barn for the evening milking. Having hooked up number 209 to the milking machine, I was leaning my choice-challenged head on the docile beast when I heard a commotion and saw two men in coats and ties walking into the barn. This was as unusual as the Queen of England strolling onto a football field. It was the two coaches from Princeton.

Before I had a chance to find out why they were there, Coach Jake carefully sidled up to my favorite half-ton of bovine. He leaned toward me and said, "How would you like to join our Princeton family, Johnny?" His piercing eyes locked onto mine. His words locked onto my heart as well.

Momentarily overwhelmed by his kindness, I muffled a sob into the side of number 209. Oh my God, I thought to myself, a real family. By the time I'd unhooked the milker and shaken Coach Jake's hand, I had regained my composure and what we called a huge "shit-eating" grin.

The decision was made. I was going to become a Princeton Tiger. It was the word "family" that made the difference. I told them I *did* want to join "the Princeton family." Nothing mattered as much to an orphan as being part of a true family. To feel like you mattered. As frightening as it was to permanently go over the wall of our Home, I now felt I would find a new home in Princeton, New Jersey.

Making this momentous decision eased the difficult transition I was about to make. As much as I yearned for freedom from the institution, Milton Hershey School with all its rules and regulations, good and bad, was all I knew. It was Home and had been Home since I could remember. As some seniors were gloating good riddance, I began to grow nostalgic as I went through the final days and weeks in Hershey.

Then in late May, I was ordered to report to the superintendent's office. The "Super" was more myth than man. He appeared from time to time at an assembly, but he was not someone HomeGuys saw on a regular basis. I was curious but assumed it had something to do with commencement when I would deliver the welcome address for my class. I was ushered into an enormous, formal office. The school psychologist and the headmaster were already seated waiting for my arrival. That startled me.

Dr. John O. Hershey was not related to Mr. Hershey but had been at the school for decades. He opened by congratulating me on my decision to go to Princeton. I started to say that the credit went to my teachers but Dr. Hershey interrupted and said that they were here about something else. They wanted to share with me some important information about my family history. That made me think the meeting was about Frankie.

The superintendent began to read from a file. He did not look up. He said that there were things about my family history that the school chose not to reveal to me for my own good. They understood my family in Snow Shoe had kept them secret as well. He said that as I was about to embark on my own, they thought I needed to know.

Both puzzled and mesmerized, I had no idea what he was talking about.

The school psychologist seemed very uncomfortable and said something like the school had decided Frankie and I were too young to constructively process traumatic information about the tragedy.

Now I was really confused. Surely they knew my parents died in a car crash back then?

Dr. Hershey cleared his throat and said he intended to read a statement without interruption. I nodded okay but felt that the whole thing was getting creepy.

He said that my parents did not die in an automobile accident. The accident was a cover story made up to protect me and Frankie. In fact, my mother had died as a result of a homicide, and my father, who was convicted of that crime, had been sentenced to life in prison. My father was serving a life sentence and had attempted to contact me during my high-school years, but the school had believed that it would be detrimental to my "health" to know about my father. Dr. Hershey ended by saying the school had been holding recent mail from my father, which they would give to me after the meeting.

I was dazed. I had dozens of questions but everything jumbled together in my mind. Homicide? My father was alive? They were "protecting" me? I had mail from my father? And where was he?

When I could speak, I blurted, "Whoa!" but before I could ask a question, Dr. Hershey stood up to signal the end of the meeting. I was dismissed. He pointed me toward the door, saying the psychologist would answer my questions and give me my mail.

I was not about to leave so quickly.

"Hold on," I said. "Our father has been alive this whole time? How could you keep that from us? Where is he? What do you mean by homicide?"

He made no effort to answer my questions but tried to hurry me out the door. My body moved toward the door but my brain remained. I was programmed to follow adult authority. But before I left, I turned and mumbled something like "Do you know that tampering with the mail is a federal offense?" The three of them looked shocked. I drew faint satisfaction from the stunned look on their faces.

I demanded my father's letters as soon as I walked into the psychologist's office. She officiously said she was ordered to answer my questions first before handing over the mail. I was about to blow a gasket, and that surge of almost unstoppable emotion felt pretty scary. By then, I was skilled at repressing all highly charged emotions. But this was uncharted waters. I coached myself to calm down and think, but my mind was speeding as fast as my feelings were surging. I breathed deeply, unclenched my fists, and forced myself to slow and settle down.

In response to my questions, the psychologist told me my father was at Rockview Penitentiary in Centre County serving a life sentence. The prison was not far from Snow Shoe. I remembered I had passed the prison on the way to a drive-in theater in Snow Shoe the previous summer. She said the earliest letters to me were dated 1958, three years ago.

I wanted to scream "How could you not tell us?" but instead, as calmly as I could, I asked, "How much did Frankie know about all this?"

She said that school officials believed he had a partial memory of the "incident" and that this partial memory contributed to his "problem." "Being there when your mother was . . ."

The idea that my father had killed my mother was simply beyond comprehension. I did not want to know anymore and instinctively my hands flew up to cover my ears until I realized how childish I must look. My mind cast about for another narrative: I wondered if my father had gotten drunk and killed my mother in a car accident. That was still terrible, but everyone had accidents.

So I asked if my mother died in a car accident.

She spoke carefully and deliberately: "It was no car accident. And yes, your brother was there and so were you. It wasn't an accident." Her voice quivered.

I put words to the horror. "You mean my father k-k-killed our mother intentionally? And Frankie and I were both there at the m-m- . . . scene?" I could not bring myself to say "murder," and my own voice shook badly.

She nodded nervously and I erupted. "Almighty God! Lord save us! How could that be? How could he? How could you not tell us?"

I needed to get away. I popped up like a jackrabbit in the Spring Creek pasture and asked for my letters so I could find some private space to absorb this daymare. She was about to object. The superintendent had been quite specific on his instructions that I read the letters in her presence so she could answer more of my "questions," but the poor woman could see I was not to be denied.

After I left her office, I could barely look at another HomeGuy, let alone speak to one, so I pretended to sleep on the activity bus taking students back to the farmhomes. I waited until after chores and dinner to take out the letters in the study room, now empty of students at this late date in May. I used a copy of *Life* magazine to hide the letters in case someone entered the room while I read. I was not about to share these letters with anyone just yet. I pulled out the first envelope.

I noticed it had been opened already and cursed the school and my handlers, then I spotted a hand-stamped message on the card inside: *Contents read and censored by authorized RP personnel.* Rockview Penitentiary personnel. My father lived under more constraints than I did. He was in a real prison.

I pulled out a card. On the front and back of the card, my father had drawn a picture of Frankie and me with colored pencils. It was quite good and fairly accurate. At the bottom, he had written, "My sons—Frankie and Johnny." Tears filled my eyes. My own father, a father I did not know I had, had drawn these likenesses. The card said,

Dear Frankie and Johnny,

I love you and miss you. Someday soon we will all be together again. Enjoy the pictures.

God bless you,
Dad

The next card was from Christmas of 1959 and included pictures of angels and a crude manger scene he had drawn. It was addressed to both of us. I wondered if he even knew Frankie was in a state hospital.

The third piece was in a standard letter-sized envelope. Our father wrote,

I was sorry to hear about Frankie. They tell me he is in Hollidaysburg, but I also hear you are doing well in your sports and school work. Good for you. Keep up the good work.

I work out and pray for you and Frankie every day. I hope they allow you to read this letter. If so, please write.

God bless you Son,
Dad

The final letter from my father was dated only three weeks earlier. He wrote,

I am proud of your accomplishments at the Hershey School. You can see I kept track of all your football games and some baseball too. I especially liked that you won the Golden Shoe!

I read in the paper that you are going to Princeton University. I have never heard of it, but they said it is a great college. Son, I would like to be at your high school graduation, but I can't. Please write soon and come visit me once you are out of the orphanage? God bless you, son.

Love,
    Dad

Love, Dad? Just like that? How dare he pretend to be a loving father after killing our mother and dooming his sons to an orphanage. The envelope included a folded enclosure. It was the Spartan football schedule copied out in his neat hand with the score of each game. He circled the two historic wins against Lancaster and Cedar Cliff, and below each game, he listed my touchdowns and measly extra points. He had written, "Batting average as of May 7, 1961: .423!" I was captain of the baseball team as a senior.

The dates showed he had kept writing to me despite no response for three years. I could not process any more. I was spent. Shock, anger, and utter confusion drained my mind and spirit. I did not want to give the school officials a shred of credit for withholding this information from us for so many years, but they were right: the knowledge was devastating. From having no recollection of my parents to reading words written to me by my father and learning he was alive and just a few hours away from me left me as empty as an upended milk bucket. His role in the death of our mother was simply more than I could fathom.

I needed help to deal with these revelations of secrets, cover-ups, and horrors but I could not rely on the school officials. Instead, I went to my favorite teacher and my favorite coach. Mr. Bickle and his wife advised me to proceed cautiously and maybe send my father a note. Coach Klingler was a risk taker. He offered to take me to the prison to visit my father the very next weekend.

I shared the information with Percy and Carmen. My friends agreed that my father must have cared if he checked the statistics in the newspaper every week for an entire year. That impressed me more than his words. Yet I was not ready to visit the parent who stole my childhood and ended the life of my mother. Throughout all of this, no one mentioned her. How could no one mention my mom?

I also needed to get through my final days as a student at Milton Hershey School. Like other graduating seniors, I experienced a jumble of conflicting emotions. We were thrilled at the notion of permanently going over the wall. Freedom to do anything we wanted was just days away. On the other hand, most of us were absolutely terrified by the prospect of leaving the familiar for the unknown. We covered up our fears with false bravado; ribbing one another mercilessly, mocking the school and its officials, and bragging about the girls, cigarettes, beer, and adventure just days away.

The reality of completing the Spartan grind was far grittier. The isolation of institutional life was so great that at least half of the graduating seniors had a "rent-a-date" for the senior prom. Most of the college-bound seniors would end up at the community college in town. The school deliberately placed graduating seniors in jobs far away from Hershey and near their hometowns or got them signed up for military service. The job-placement service conspired to keep graduates far away to stop the wily veterans from corrupting and influencing the kids still in the school.

When HomeGuys graduated, we were on our own in every way, ill-prepared orphans bobbing in a lifeboat in the midst of churning ocean seas. We were supposed to figure everything out after living for years in an environment where every decision was made for us. We were free but confused, like a herd of Holsteins released from their stalls in the middle of the night. Where do you go? What do you do? How do you decide? From 100 percent regimented to 100 percent free in the space of two minutes was so disorienting I felt as though I were watching myself acting in a scene from a play.

The school had given us roots but not wings. Some of us, lifers mostly, had literally nowhere to go or stay once over the wall. I luckily had a sweet girlfriend, Patty, a sophomore from Hershey whom I had been dating for some time. I'd had brief flings with a few local girls who were my age and were way too fast for me. Like all but a few Home-Guys, assertive girls scared my pants off (or rather, more tightly on). Girls were as foreign to HomeGuys as a two-legged cow. Patty, on the other hand, was a safe and perfect fit for me.

My grandmother and other relatives had driven to my graduation from Snow Shoe, and they left to make the long drive back. Coach Jake from Princeton showed up, an unexpected delight, but he left as well. I had nowhere to go or stay. Fortunately, my girlfriend Patty's family offered me a place to stay that night.

Not all my classmates were as fortunate. Some slept in a borrowed car. A few snuck back and slept in the haylofts of the old barns. Two had the nerve to break into the rear entrance of Old Senior Hall and camp out in the sports-equipment room for several weeks.

Even then as a raw seventeen year old, I understood that it was wrong for the school to send us into the world this way with so little preparation. It was my job to deliver the senior class Welcome Address. I would have liked to have addressed this grievous shortcoming in the system, a shortcoming that has been replicated for decades in a foster-care system that tosses kids out of care at the age of eighteen whether they are ready or not. I would have liked to have suggested in my speech that the school give older orphans more freedom and more chances to make decisions to prepare them better for life after graduation. But I had been trained here to go along and not make waves and to do anything but this at that time would have gotten my wonderful English teacher and speech coach in trouble.

Upon my leaving Milton Hershey School, three things stood out for me. The first was my brother's tragic journey, which ended up in a horrible mental institution. Perhaps this was a bit of survivor's guilt. My big brother had been lost, I was saved. Whatever the cause, Frankie was on my mind constantly. The contrast between his Milton Hershey School journey ending in despair and mine ending at an Ivy League college seemed brutally unfair to me.

The second highlight was the amazing bonds of brotherhood and perseverance shared by HomeGuys. I later learned that boys develop similar bonds at high-end boarding schools. But we orphan boys had shared a grittier, harder path that made our loyalty to one another an unbreakable, lifelong connection. Part of me understood that I would never be truly alone because my HomeGuy best friends would always be brothers. It proved to be true.

The third factor was that the Class of 1961 had done something truly extraordinary. We were leaving Milton Hershey School a safer, more respectful place for kids of all sizes and stripes. We had broken the back of the bullying system by refusing to perpetuate it when we became the big guys. It was not completely eradicated. There was still bullying at some farmhomes. But for the most part, my pals and I had helped to stop the practice of making little guys "personal slaves." To become widespread again, the practice would have to be reintroduced and reinvented.

Yet I also understood that we had not completely succeeded. I knew there were members of our class who were humiliated and hounded only because they did not fit the HomeGuy mold. They were "different": less macho, less tough, more, dare I say, like my gentle big brother Frankie. Their unique qualities invited torment in the closed, all-boy world of thrown-away children.

I did my last milking on graduation day. Walking out to the dairy barn at Spring Creek in my dung-encrusted dungarees for the last time, a tug-of-war erupted in me between wanting to get it over with as quickly as I could and wanting to savor every last second. I had hustled out to the barn thousands of times in the frozen darkness of winter mornings and on sweaty, humid summer afternoons. In two hours, I would walk away forever.

Part of me said good riddance and was relieved to be spared the grind of daily barnwork. But I knew I would miss the simple beauty of our Dutch barn that sheltered animals who had shared in this grind. The Holsteins and manure had become part of me, as intrinsic to me as my eye and hair color. The daily chores and the productivity from working hard every day at physically grueling tasks had taught me what it means to have a purpose in life. It was not easy to admit this at the time, but I did. Even then I realized I had been saved by Milton Hershey School. I knew I owed the school a huge debt. Little did I know that many years later, I would get a chance to repay it.

7

MILTON HERSHEY SCHOOL DRIFTS OFF MISSION

A 10,000-acre campus becomes a Town Center. *Courtesy of the Milton Hershey School*

Many members of the newly minted Class of 1961 did go off with the remnants of their families that night. But many stayed in Hershey after commencement to experience what this town and campus would feel like to a free man. Most of the lifers stayed. After fourteen years in our Home, we really had no other place to go. But it was clear that the school was done with us far more than we were done with her.

Patty's dad loaned me their family station wagon for a "boy's night out" if I promised not to drink. For me, that was an easy promise to make and keep. Moreover, my pals had scattered. It was still a school night for Patty, and she had to turn in early. So I drove the station wagon two blocks to Chocolate Avenue where the candy factory loomed and something besides the "four on the column," something in me, shifted.

My spirit soared. Driving a car, on my own, late at night, outside the reach of the Spartan authorities was exhilarating, maybe intoxicating, but I wouldn't know about that at the time. I had traversed these same streets a thousand times in our yellow school buses cheering "Rooty toot toot" and "Brown and Gold" since back in kindergarten. In that spirit, I began tooting the horn at the few night revelers I spotted. They must have thought I was crazy. They were right. I was deliriously happy. I was free. Here I was still smack in the middle of Hershey. But I had chosen to be here in this place at this time, honking my freaking horn. On my own. I felt as though I had vaulted over a whole bunch of walls.

Freedom, however, was not completely free. The thrill came with a commensurate level of anxiety. In the days leading up to my enrollment at Princeton in 1961, I became so scared and excited that I could barely eat. The reality of going from a humble orphanage to a prestigious Ivy League university felt overwhelming. I had that cocky, HomeGuy swagger down pat, but I wondered if I hadn't gotten in over my head as I rode onto the Princeton campus in a friend's beat-up old Chevy.

Princeton University is one of the nine original Colonial colleges, founded in 1746 before the American Revolution (Princeton was briefly capital of the nation during the Revolution). The university created its own bucolic and self-contained world on five hundred acres in central New Jersey, about an hour between New York City and Philadelphia. The stone Gothic buildings, literally covered by ivy, give the campus a timeless elegance and grace. Man-made Lake Carnegie anchors one end of campus. Andrew Carnegie financed the lake's construction at the request of a Princeton graduate friend. He hoped to encourage the students to take up rowing and give up football, which he viewed as an ungentlemanly sport. Princeton did not take the bait, to my eternal gratitude. In fact, Princeton played the first game of intercollegiate football, facing Rutgers University in 1869, and has produced a proud and winning tradition for almost 150 years.

Dick "Percy" Purcell, my lifelong Milton Hershey School friend, pulled his old Chevy up to 33 Little Hall, my new dorm. I carried all my worldly goods in a half-empty green Army duffle bag. Most of my clothes had been destroyed in an unfortunate car accident earlier that summer. I still had most of the $100 cash gift that Milton Hershey's deed of trust bestowed on every graduating senior. The contrast between my modest arrival and that of many of my classmates could not have been more stark or dramatic. Percy and I were surrounded by Mercedes Benz station wagons and other European imports foreign to me. I spotted a limousine driven by a chauffeur. I had never seen a chauffeur before. My jaw dropped in amazement. Students and parents hauled sofas, television sets, refrigerators, and typewriters into the dorms like dutiful lines of busy ants heading into a nest.

I grabbed my pathetic, second-hand duffle bag and asked Percy if I had missed some "what to bring" memo. A rare surge of panic took hold. "I don't think I can do this," I murmured. Percy calmly insisted I could, and he told me to go find my roommates, who included Cosmo Iacavazzi, the high-school football star from Scranton and my teammate during the Pennsylvania All Star game.

The four-man suite was quite a contrast to our tiny Milton Hershey School bedrooms, but my new roommates were as warm and earthy as the best Spartan brothers I knew. Cosmo was a fierce competitor on the gridiron, and we forged a friendship that has lasted our entire lives. And Ron and Mike, my other suitemates, and Cosmo all came from circumstances nearly as impoverished as my own. If they could do Princeton, then I must surely try.

Princeton was loaded with students from far more privileged backgrounds than mine. But my initial concerns about the differences proved to be baseless. The cultural, social, and economic differences between us were huge but not readily apparent on campus. We all wore the same casual clothes, almost a uniform of khakis or chinos and sweatshirts or faded polo shirts. Everyone dressed down. It was a comfortable and collegial, all-male, very white environment. No doubt we all would have benefited from a more diverse student body, but it was a different time. Coeducation, affirmative action, and an appreciation of the educational benefits of diversity lay in the future.

I never experienced the elitist F. Scott Fitzgerald version of Princeton. I could never even tell the prep school kids from the public school kids. In fact, I was so oblivious to class and cultural differences that I did not realize one of my roommates, Rich, was Jewish until I visited his parents at their New York City penthouse apartment a year later. To me, he was another extremely bright, kind, and wonderful guy among hundreds of bright, kind, and wonderful guys. I only remember one time that a classmate bragged about his wealth and ancestry, and that was through an alcoholic haze after his girlfriend dumped him. I do remember having to tune out when some innocent pre-holiday conversations featured Europe or islands or skiing somewhere. Selective hearing was already one of my survival skills. Overall, my Princeton classmates were terrific young men: open, accepting, friendly, funny, and very smart.

Once again football helped keep me alive. The football team formed its own unique, close-knit subculture. Once we suited up in the familiar gear of gridiron combat and hit the practice field, I felt right at home. I had played tailback at Milton Hershey and wanted to play that position on Princeton's single-wing offense, but twelve other freshmen had the same idea. I realized I was now a minnow in a big surging ocean. However, my intensity, focus, and persistence, all honed at Milton Hershey School, proved to be an enormous advantage for me. I became starting tailback for the freshman team, and we won all but one game. But more important to me than playing time was finding a new family. Football facilitates the bonds of friendship fast and deep because football requires full immersion; you have to sacrifice yourself completely on every play. Shared adversity at that level builds lifelong bonds.

My first year of academic performance did not go nearly as well. Some of my Milton Hershey School teachers had decided I should major in engineering. "It is your patriotic duty, Johnny, now that the Russians have put Sputnik in orbit," opined Mr. Bickle. I did well in all my studies at Milton Hershey School, and my teachers reasoned that the employment opportunities for young engineers and scientists would be excellent at the beginning of the 1960s when the arms competition with the Soviet Union was at its peak. I really had no other career counseling, so I agreed. As a first-year engineering major at Princeton, I was required to take advanced calculus, engineering physics, and chemistry. Economics 101, Shakespeare, and a writing tutorial rounded out my first-semester class work.

From the start, calculus and advanced physics left me utterly baffled. I had no idea what the professors were talking about, no matter how hard I listened. I studied intensely and my friends tried to help me, but the harder I studied and the more intently I listened, the murkier the subject matter became. The midterm test results were disastrous, so I studied harder and got more help. I could at least understand *King Lear*, which resonated with my own experience with human suffering, and I quickly grasped basic economic concepts, so those two classes went well. Then final exams came.

For the mind-boggling calculus exam, I jotted down all the equations I had memorized the night before during a desperate, final, all-night study frenzy. I got the Princeton equivalent of an F-. The physics exam was worse. It had just two questions. The first, worth 70 percent of the grade, was about calculating the speed and vector of an insect on the sail of a boat if the boat was moving at a speed of x miles per hour while the wind was moving at a speed of y miles per hour in a z direction with the tide moving at b miles per hour in an a direction. I read that question ten times. Then I drew a pretty pathetic picture of the sailboat and turned in my exam booklet. I flunked.

After getting nothing but 1s (or As) in high school, this failure was devastating. I went into a stupor of confusion and denial for a week until I got a notice from the Dean's office that I was on academic probation. Now I was depressed and ashamed. I started to think I should go to a less-competitive school; maybe Princeton was just too hard for a HomeGuy from Hershey. Maybe Penn State will still have me, I thought. Or maybe I should just limp back to Hershey Junior College and be with my HomeGuy buddies.

My roommates rallied me. You're not a quitter, Johnny, they said. The word "quitter" pierced my heart like a knife. Coach Jake also intervened. He spoke to my professors and found out that I was doing just fine in economics and literature. He told me that Princeton would never have admitted me if the university had thought I was not capable of doing the academic work, and then he told me the obvious: I did not have to major in engineering.

Coach Jake said, "You just can't be an engineer, Johnny. Let the rest of these brainiacs be the engineers." He waved an expansive arm at my brainy roommates. We cracked up laughing and relief coursed through my veins like milk through a Surge milking machine. Eventually, I shifted my major to psychology, a subject I found engrossing. I suppose growing up in an orphanage, being the product of a dysfunctional family, having a brother with a severe mental illness, and having a father incarcerated in prison for life made me curious about the human mind and psyche. One of my favorite takeaways from my major came from British psychiatrist R. D. Laing, who said, "Neurosis can be a wonderful thing compared to adjustment which can be the worst possible sin leading to all kinds of conformity." Milton Hershey had been all about "adjustment." Princeton invited "creative neurosis." I wanted to understand myself, my background, and all these wonderfully strange people I was meeting as well.

Milton Hershey School had literally saved my life. I felt a debt to Milton Hershey School. But Princeton gave me an exceptional educational foundation for the rest of my life journey. When I first began scouting out colleges, I made academics a priority. I knew I would never be a professional athlete. I also understood at some very basic level that my education would be a crucial determinant for the rest of my life. This attitude proved to be prescient. At Princeton my career as a student athlete started strong but then faltered. I remained a committed member of the football team yet played less over time as injuries took a toll on my body.

My ego suffered badly from my being moved from tailback to wingback and then from starter to a mere substitute by senior year. And being on the bench in 1964, the year Princeton fielded one of its best teams ever, and the university's last undefeated team, was tough. Yet the cohesion and teamwork I learned at Milton Hershey remained part of me. While envious, I cheered my teammates from the sideline, and the lessons I learned earlier about leadership were reinforced by Coach Colman, the brains; Coach Jake, the spirit; and Captain Cosmo, the heart. They turned an ordinary group of athletes into an extraordinarily united force by setting high expectations, demanding hard work, and imbuing the team with an indomitable spirit.

The Princeton team my senior year just could not lose. During one late season game we were tied with Yale, also undefeated, at halftime.

Coach Colman, not known for his locker room speeches, sensed the tension in the room and risked a rallying cry. It was a classic.

"OK lads," he cried, "so we gave them a score at the close of the half they did not deserve—fiddle dee dee! So we're tied. That's not so bad. I mean worse things have happened . . ."

He hesitated, searching for an example. You could practically see his mind pulsing. Then he blurted out, "Lincoln was shot!"

The Tiger locker room erupted in hoots, howls, and hysterical laughter. Lincoln was shot! Talk about a non sequitur! A more relaxed and confident team returned to the playing field. Cosmo reeled off two long touchdown runs, and the Bulldogs did not have a chance. We won 35-14 and seized the Ivy League Championship on national television before sixty thousand shrieking fans at the Yale Bowl. I learned a lot from observing that masterful triumph.

One crucial lesson I absorbed is what is now known as "servant leadership." Feeling somewhat useless on the bench, I was gradually getting good at being supportive of my teammates. It was hard to get past my jealousy and personal ego needs, but my need to contribute in whatever way I could won out. I was able to use this understanding of the power of positive reinforcement and inspiration later in coaching corporate executives and then when I returned home to Milton Hershey School as its president.

Once I got into an academic major that suited me, I thrived in the rich education pool of Princeton and went from academic probation to being a B+ student by my senior year. My freshman year academic meltdown taught me a lot about humility and showed me that I would probably always be up against someone who was smarter, quicker, and more accomplished. While I was beginning to learn that resilience and adaptability could keep me competitive, I also realized that part of me remained as rigid and unyielding as the rules at Milton Hershey School and that I would spend the rest of my life trying to find the sweet spot between toughness and vulnerability.

Princeton also taught me how to think. I could come up with factual answers in high school, but I had no capacity to properly analyze and seek solutions to problems in a disciplined manner. I learned how to do that at Princeton, where I was constantly required to apply rigor to my thinking and writing and, going one step further, to engage in original thinking, using my own unique views, to answer tough questions in a creative way. I loved this. Princeton actually valued my opinions, and I had plenty to share. And its crowning project, the senior thesis, allowed me to do an original research study, "Creativity and the Flexibility of Thinking in Children." I conducted the study with Milton Hershey School grade-school kids and with a Milton Hershey School career vaguely in mind.

Princeton also helped me process my new family identity. In those first years after the shock of learning of my father's existence, I could not bring myself to do more than write him an occasional note, usually around the holidays. I could not forgive him for killing my mother and for robbing me and Frankie of a normal childhood. I did not want to see him. He was a monster who murdered our mother and abandoned us. Yet time and maturity brought perspective. As I took courses like Deviant Personality and Prisoner Culture and Rehabilitation, I gained some insight into the dysfunction of my own family. Eventually, I realized that I needed to forgive my father for my own sake.

In 1968, three years after graduating from Princeton, I was hanging with my HomeGuys in Hershey when they reminded me it was time to meet my father. It was difficult to say no to my brothers, especially Percy and Tony. And by then, I felt it was right; I needed to face this man who gave me life but also profoundly changed my life. Tony made it easier by accompanying me on that first trip. My heart and mind played ping-pong on the ride to Rockview Penitentiary. I was in a rush of dread and excitement, and wonder and angst, as well as fear and hope.

I was shocked upon first seeing my father. Aside from the obvious difference in age, we looked exactly the same. We had the same strong, jutting O'Brien jaw, the same squared-off face, the same light blue eyes, the same balding forehead and big O'Brien smile. I thought he would look like a monster. Instead, he looked just like me.

He pulled out a scrapbook that not only chronicled my Milton Hershey sports history, but my Princeton years as well. He knew Princeton had been undefeated and ranked twelfth in the nation. It was overwhelming. I could not yet embrace him as my father. I had too many reservations, and his apparent affection for me just seemed like too much, too fast, and too glib. At the time I mumbled a thank you for his interest.

After several more visits, I found that I liked this stranger, and I decided to help my father "go over the wall": to get out of prison. Something troubled me about the story of my mother's death and his role in it. He had been sentenced to life in prison for first-degree murder, but what I knew about the tragedy and what I knew about the law did not square. I got a good pro bono attorney from a big Philadelphia firm through the Princeton network and finally learned the facts of my mother's murder from my father's original trial transcript. My hands literally trembled and my stomach clenched as I opened the transcript. This document contained the answers to many questions and to some questions I could not even articulate. This is what I learned.

My parents had been at Grandpa O'Brien's home the night my mother prepared to leave our father and her marriage. The marriage was troubled, and my father evidently had a problem with his temper and with drinking. They argued violently, and our father, in a not-uncommon alcoholic haze, pulled a pistol from his pickup truck and shot our mother at close range. He then called the police and asked for an ambulance. Our mother died of her wounds soon after arriving at the hospital. Our father was taken into custody and then convicted.

Finally, I knew the source of the loud pops, screams, and blood of the nightmares Frankie and I had experienced. We had been there after all. Heaven help us. Help Frankie at least. Is this what the school psychologist was trying to tell us when they finally revealed "the secret" at Hershey? That we were there? And that Frankie, at age four, likely remembered all of it? Oh, sweet Jesus.

But I realized eventually that the murder was not premeditated. Murderers typically do not call for help after killing someone. My lawyer was outraged when he discovered that my father was assigned an inept, court-appointed attorney. We appealed to the governor's office for a review of my father's sentence. He had already served twenty-seven years in a maximum security prison, far longer than the length of time required for a conviction on a fairer charge. The correctional authorities claimed that he was too institutionally fragile to ever be released. But we got him sprung after Percy helped arrange a job and housing for him in Hershey. My dad went over the wall in the summer of 1972, about the same time I became a father for the first time myself.

My father proved to be a highly flawed man. In later years, I would say I'd become the father of two at the same time: my infant son Jason and my father. My dad was "institutionally fragile," and he had psychological issues that contributed to the crime that put him there. I accepted him for what he was, but it took a while to truly forgive him. The real reconciliation took place several years after his release when I finally told him how terrifying it had been to be abandoned, how angry I was about his inability to protect Frankie, and how hollow and alone I felt for many long years trying to prove I was loveable. It was a difficult conversation and we both cried. To be that honest and forgive someone who has hurt you that deeply is so hard. Yet it freed and refreshed me. I did it as much for my own sake as his because nothing is more corrosive than anger, resentment, and bitterness. Life is too short.

After graduating from Princeton, my first real job was teaching and coaching at a boarding school in Marion, Massachusetts. Tabor Academy is nestled next to a beautiful harbor on Buzzards Bay across from Cape Cod. I taught math and English, coached three sports, co-mastered a dorm, and helped with admissions and the dining hall. Those of us on the faculty figured we earned about 63 cents an hour. I loved it. As I worked with young people who were seeking, questioning, experimenting, and growing, I was too. I was hooked on human growth, including my own, since I was a rough work-in-progress. And I learned something that surprised me. In some ways, those privileged prep school kids were as emotionally needy as the orphans of Hershey. Many of these kids felt abandoned too after being dropped off at school in September and then shipped off to summer camp in June, despite the affluence of their parents. Like orphans, they were little sump pumps of need, endlessly seeking approval and validation.

Other faculty members cautioned me that Tabor was like an addictive drug and so intoxicating that I might wake up one day twenty-five years hence and find I had never been anywhere else. In my twenties, I still burned with many ambitions. I had married a girl, Connie, I met in Hershey right after graduating from Princeton, and as much as I enjoyed teaching, I was still not certain that classroom teaching was my destiny. So I left Tabor to attend graduate school at Johns Hopkins in Baltimore. For the second time, I turned down a Harvard offer of admissions, which I gleefully tease my Harvard colleagues about. I did not actually feel very smart about that, but I agreed with my wife that we would save money by living with her parents in Maryland.

The tether to Milton Hershey School remained as strong as ever. I returned for Homecomings and reunions with my buddies, my brothers, my HomeGuys. With my childhood now distant in the rear-view mirror, the memories of my youth became softer, more nostalgic. I began to tease out the good things more and more and to shelve many of the bad memories. After earning a master's degree in education at Johns Hopkins, I applied for a rare opening in the admissions office at Princeton. But out of the blue, a senior Milton Hershey School administrator called me to ask if I was interested in coming back to teach and coach for the Spartans.

Interested? I was interested and honored and eager to return with the knowledge I had gained to improve my old Home. I wanted to help diversify enrollment, and I wanted to propose some sort of independent-living program to give older students a taste of freedom before being dumped into independence on graduation day.

The offer was to teach English and Health and be the head football coach. By the time I formally applied for the position, the duties also included being the Director of Religious Education. That gave me a momentary pause because I was not particularly religious and still felt far too young and too wild to be serving as a moral role model for children.

When the formal offer arrived, I was so ecstatic that I immediately wrote an acceptance letter. The letter brimmed with gratitude and appreciation, and I even asked if I could start earlier. I was so anxious to get back. In my closing paragraph, I mentioned a few areas where I thought I could improve the Milton Hershey School experience for both students and staff. I called it an effort to "help make a good place even better."

Four days later, Milton Hershey School rescinded the job offer. Stunned to the core, I reread the letter from the headmaster over and over. What had I done to offend them so? Upon reflection, I realized that I had become a staunch idealist at Princeton. I believed anything was possible, and like so many idealistic young people, I was tilting at windmills. I wanted to charge on my white horse, but I was a bit oblivious to practical problems. Had I been too idealistic, too passionate, too outspoken in my acceptance letter? Maybe I needed to learn to be more politic and more strategic in making recommendations for change. Despite my deep disappointment, I worked through it and concluded that I did not really want to be at a place that could not tolerate a little bit of constructive, heartfelt feedback. I remembered the sacred Milton Hershey School Pledge: "I will keep my standards high and help others do likewise." I took it to heart. I would stay true to my ideals.

I did land the Princeton job. I joked that it was not a bad second choice! My formative years on the staff of Princeton University admissions included the upheavals brought about by nonstop antiwar demonstrations and the sweeping social and cultural changes of the 1960s. I had a hard time coming to terms with those demonstrations. It took me a while to appreciate that not every student was overwhelmed by gratitude at the opportunity to attend what I considered the world's best university. It never occurred to me that students might have deeply held principles and enough conviction to openly challenge sacred authority. Unlike MHS, Princeton tolerated major dissent.

My time in that job also coincided with Princeton's decision to admit women and go coed. Like most graduates who loved their school just the way it was, I initially hated the idea of women at Princeton. But I was a member of a coeducation task force, and the data we received overwhelmingly favored a Princeton open to all who qualified on merit. I also gained an acute appreciation for the rich benefits of racial and gender diversity in a student body as I labored with my admissions colleagues to make that first coed class as broad, bright, and promising as my alma mater deserved. Since we were only admitting a small number of trailblazing women, every decision was critical.

Eventually, after working for the National Institute of Education, I went into business for myself at the end of the 1970s and founded Renaissance Leadership, a consulting practice that coached corporate executives on effective leadership. My first marriage had ended, and I took some time to come to terms with that failure and my own role in it and the adjustment to absentee parenthood. By then, we had two children, Jason and Kelly, both terrific kids.

It took almost a full year and my life savings to land my first major client, Smith Barney. I was 0 for 63 on my first sales calls to Fortune 500 companies. George Wilder, the training director at Smith Barney and a Princeton grad, decided to take a risk on me. Through him, I landed a contract to work with the new Smith Barney account executives for the next year and then for years to follow. That contract led to others with AT&T, Colgate Palmolive, Pfizer, American Express, and Glaxo Smith Kline. Many stayed with us for more than a decade, a few for twenty years. The four virtues of accountability, transparency, authenticity, and vulnerability were at the heart of Renaissance Leadership philosophy and program design. We taught our clients how to internalize these principles to make real and lasting culture change at their companies. I also blundered into a puzzling phenomenon. The more we charged for our service, the more valuable our clients perceived it, and our client list grew.

Throughout the years, I was always thinking about Milton Hershey School and how the lessons I had learned and was teaching to others could be applied to my old home. I kept in touch with my fellow Home-Guys, and during the 1970s, I served on the board of the Milton Hershey School Alumni Association. I rarely missed Homecoming and I relished the reunions with old pals. We immediately reverted to the sophomoric teasing on who was getting a little fat and who was losing more hair (that was usually me), and we returned to the mocking nicknames, like "manure breath," that we used as kids. I am not ashamed to admit that we still tease one another mercilessly even as grandfathers now looking toward our eighth decade.

My old German teacher, Herr Fisher, was now President Fisher of Milton Hershey School. During the 1988 Homecoming, he inquired about my consulting business and asked me to send a proposal for consulting services for his senior team, which was then laboring under considerable stress. After all those years, I facilitated a three-day workshop for President Fisher and his management team at a retreat on the Chesapeake Bay.

I familiarized myself with the current issues at Milton Hershey School. Much of the stress on President Fisher and his team came from differences with the board of managers. The board existed in an echo chamber, and outsiders rarely broke into the clique. Indeed, the first woman did not join the board of managers until 1984. So it was almost inevitable that the board members would convince themselves that they knew best. The board of managers had absolute power. As British historian Lord Acton wrote long ago, "Power tends to corrupt, and absolute power corrupts absolutely."

When Mr. Hershey was alive and his handpicked associates formed the board, there was unanimity of purpose that reflected the founder's views and vision. By the end of the 1980s, however, some on the board began to question the practice of serving only the neediest children. The board had commissioned a marketing study in 1988 to make the school more attractive to prospective students, and they wanted the rapid changes called for in that study implemented. But President Fisher and his staff were convinced Milton Hershey School was in essentially good shape and thought gradual change more appropriate.

The Fisher team had finally ended the school's dependency on the dairy-farm system. This was a huge, historic step. I must note that graduates who were barn guys and the pioneering barn girls viewed this change very differently from those who never had to dung out a barn in smelly dungarees at 5 a.m. Most of the barn guys believed Milton Hershey School lost its soul when the Holsteins were sold. Of course, these same guys despised the grueling oppression of their own daily farm life, but these things are rarely logical. What struck and concerned all alumni was that the absence of the daily work demands of the farms began to erode the famous Milton Hershey School work ethic. Training that fostered the ability to work long and hard distinguished Milton Hershey School graduates from students at other schools. That work ethic also gave the orphan students who had so little a real shot at surviving and thriving in adulthood. Nothing is more American. Penniless immigrants have come to the United States for generations with nothing more than hope and heart and have succeeded beyond their own dreams simply because they worked hard.

There is no question that ending the dairy program was a major change, but most of the other changes being put into effect by President Fisher and his team were incremental. The board wanted far more sweeping change, what they called their 21st Century Initiative. That is when the troubles began. Given the extraordinary power held by the board and the lack of any real counterweight to that power, conflict was inevitable.

President Fisher could see that he was out of step with the board. He hailed from the old school and believed deeply in the mission of Milton-Hershey School. He had come up through the ranks as a teacher and administrator and probably understood Milton Hershey School better than any other person alive. As a graduate and lifelong Spartan, he not only understood the primacy of the core values of hard work, persistence, and discipline, he recognized that Milton Hershey's vision was to stretch out a helping hand to boys and girls who would otherwise be lost.

After six years as president, William R. Fisher announced his retirement in April of 1990, bowing to an insistence upon reform and changes he did not support. Fisher was as solid as a Pennsylvania limestone boulder, but the board of managers, led by a lawyer at the time, thought him inflexible and not innovative enough to lead the new era. Although the man I always thought of as "Herr" Fisher disagreed with some of the basic premises underlying the proposed changes, he retired without a fuss, two months after the board announced the long-range planning goals of the 21st Century Initiative. He said he was doing so "in the best interests of the School." It was a gracious and selfless act but also characteristic of the go-along-to-get-along mentality that was so pervasive at Milton Hershey School. People who challenged the status quo simply did not survive at the school. The culture of the place valued discipline, order, conformity, and cooperation. It could not tolerate dissent.

President Fisher had acted as a significant mentor and role model to me at Milton Hershey School. During my senior year when I was overwhelmed by my sports, leadership roles, and studies, I thought out loud in his presence about my need to get better organized. I said I hoped one day to have a briefcase as fine as his and asked if he might know someone who had an old used one they might be willing to give up. He winked and said he'd ask around. After school the next day, Bill Fisher drove me to a leather goods store in Harrisburg and bought me a brand-new briefcase that looked like his own. I was floored and tears welled up in my eyes. I did not cry. That would have been a serious violation of the HomeGuy ethic, but he knew what that gesture meant to me.

Replacing Fisher as president proved difficult, and the next four years featured a revolving door of leaders. The inability to settle on the right president contributed to the tension. The first new president, Dr. Frances O'Connor, a veteran educator who had been principal for twelve years at a private day-school in New Jersey, left after only eight months on the job. The school officials attributed her departure to something about incompatibility of style. No Milton Hershey School president had served fewer than four years. The board was clearly embarrassed and driven to find a sound replacement.

Then the board chairman, Rod J. Pera, a lawyer who was a graduate of Hershey High, took over as acting president from May 1992 until the summer of 1993. Pera was a deft inside player who had built a considerable power base in the various Hershey entities. He was on the board of Hershey Foods Corporation and Hershey Entertainment and Resorts, and he was chairman of the board of the Hershey Trust Company.

On June 17, 1993, the board announced that Dr. Arthur Levine of the Harvard Graduate School, a nationally known education expert, had agreed to be the sixth president of Milton Hershey School. Shocking everyone, however, Levine declined the offer a month later, and the basis for his decision was never disclosed beyond vaguely cited personal reasons. He never even showed up on campus.

With egg on its collective face, the board then had to scramble to find a replacement, and they rushed back to other candidates on their short list. The victor was a longtime Iowa educator, the former superintendent of schools in Council Bluffs, Dr. William Lepley. His appointment was announced on August 11, 1993. A lot happened during his tenure that affects the governance and operation of Milton Hershey School to this day. What happened just before he arrived perhaps tainted his tenure forever.

Before Lepley began his new job, Rod Pera and the board fired six popular, longtime administrators in what became dramatically known as the "Severed Six" tragedy. Looking back, it is evident that the discharge of six longtime administrators was done to clear the decks and give the incoming president the opportunity to name his own team and implement the board's agenda. But the summary firing of the half-dozen managers revealed a deep gulf between the philosophy of the board and the philosophy of Milton Hershey. There had never been a multiple firing at the school. The personal trust and respect that had governed Milton Hershey School leadership for almost ninety years was suddenly and severely eroded.

The Alumni Association reported that the school had begun accepting students with higher IQs who performed closer to grade level and who came from more-affluent families. Catering to students and their parents is something that expensive private schools, which compete with one another for tuition, may feel is necessary. It was not a great leap to realize that enrolling better-prepared and less-needy students would produce better "outcomes" of all kinds. That was what the marketing study called for. The 21st Century Initiative took these "better" students and gave them more of everything, granted them more freedom and fewer chores and other responsibilities. While this may be an appropriate strategy for a conventional private boarding school, it was not what Mr. Hershey intended.

To the HomeGuys, the board had gone too far. Poverty had not disappeared since Mr. Hershey's time. The plight of poor children was just as dire as ever. To us, culling out "the most likely to succeed" disadvantaged students and leaving behind boys and girls who came from dysfunctional families and desperate poverty completely violated the deed of trust.

For decades, the school had operated in a sweetly old-fashioned way where trust was the most important currency and a handshake sufficed to close a deal or an employment agreement. The Severed Six episode changed all that. A week after the dismissal of the six administrators, according to court documents, the faculty petitioned the Pennsylvania State Education Association for union representation; two weeks later, the house parents asked Chocolate Workers Union Local 464 to represent them. Two years later, the operations-and-support-services employees also joined Local 464.

There is nothing inherently wrong or surprising about unionization. The Hershey manufacturing company had been unionized for years. But unionization involves a different workplace mindset. In the past, the teaching staff and other employees viewed themselves as trusted members of the Milton Hershey School family with a mission so sacred that each could count on the other to be fair and honest. The new Union leaders cared more about "work rules," for example, and they made demands for changes that would make Milton Hershey School far less of a year-round Home: more vacation time, more substitute houseparents, and a ban on "triple hitting"—that great prep school practice of having your best staff teach, coach, and houseparent. "Houseparenting by contract" became the new normal.

Unionization was only one unintended consequence of the Severed Six. The student body staged a walk-out, left their classrooms at Old Senior Hall, and marched down Patt's Hill for a protest rally. Nothing like this had ever happened at Milton Hershey School. The students felt outraged over the discharge of the Severed Six but also "entitled" to have things their way. The alumni staged a protest downtown and on the school campus to denounce the firings and the 21st Century Initiative. We alumni organized an action group called Coalition of Worried Supporters (COWS), a corny but characteristic acronym that captured the mindset of the alumni better than any outsider would appreciate.

Shortly after the protests, Mr. Pera resigned and left for New Mexico. Something fundamental had changed. The deference the alumni and staff had felt toward the board was now gone after eighty years. The firing of the Severed Six affected me deeply. Like others, I was outraged. Yet I initially hesitated before publically criticizing the school I loved. I knew the consequences of speaking out against the almighty board, but in the end an innate sense of integrity and justice triumphed. I remembered that psychologist Erik Ericson had said that judicious indignation is "a core trait for good social scientists. Indignation takes on injustice." I went public along with COWS and criticized the abuse of power, the violation of Mr. Hershey's sacred trust, and the corrosive role modeling for our Spartan kids. Although I knew I had done the right thing, I felt like I had violated some sacred family norm. I also knew that I was now limited to playing a minor role for my beloved Home.

For much of the 1990s, the always hopeful and polite alumni gave President Lepley time and a chance to make things right. I give him credit for making our Home a more nurturing—less macho—place where emotional needs of students were legitimized and treated openly. He said encouraging things and engaged in a long process of studies, committees, and work groups to produce a strategic plan. One of the chief architects of this plan was a public-relations consultant from Harrisburg. This approach was reminiscent of the marketing study conducted in the late 1980s. It soon became obvious to many alumni that the new strategic plan was a carefully worded rewrite of the despised 21st Century Initiative. Disaffected staff inside the school supplied COWS with key facts. The school was enrolling less-needy kids with higher IQs and better grades. New students were closer to grade level for their age than any other applicant cohort in the history of Milton Hershey School. Very few alumni remained on the staff. The alumni representation in the workforce was cut by half within five years.

By the late 1990s, it was clear that key components of the original Hershey mission had been abandoned. Not only were the students less needy and more academically qualified, but Milton Hershey's edict that

Milton Hershey School would be "a home with a school" had been turned upside down. Holidays were added and expanded, and many kids were sent home for the entire summer. Many students were now off-campus for over four months of the year. It was very clear the school was no longer serving the neediest and most-alone children. Moreover, Milton Hershey School was not even a real home to its kids any longer. It was becoming closer to a middle-class prep school.

The Alumni Association grew restive and became more critical. In response, President Lepley created his own separate Alumni Advisory Council in what COWS viewed as a classic divide-and-conquer strategy. But that only succeeded in coalescing alumni dissent. At the same time, the school budget doubled within six years, but fewer students were being served. The school endowment had also doubled and was now hovering at $5 billion, a stunning amount of money. There is something about that type of money that attracts notice. Even the attorney general of Pennsylvania was beginning to take notice.

Given the size of the endowment, some of us thought the school should devise a strategy to serve more needy children with direct services. Mr. Lepley and his board went in a radically different direction. They proposed to take millions of dollars to create a think-tank called the Catherine Hershey Institute for Learning and Development (CHILD). They claimed that too few needy children could be found to support expanding the school enrollment. The think-tank had a nice name and a high-minded purpose: to provide research grants to develop ways to improve the teaching and parenting of needy children. But again, it was not what the founders had intended. Ultimately Judge Morgan of Dauphin County Orphan Court ruled against CHILD, finding it was "hostile" to the founder's deed of trust.

This was not the first time the board of managers had looked for other ways to spend the endowment. In 1963, just two years after my graduation, the trustees quietly took $50 million from the endowment and gave it to Penn State to create the Milton S. Hershey Medical Center, a teaching hospital. The gift represented about 20 percent of the trust's total assets. The deed of trust could be interpreted broadly, and the medical center was unquestionably an asset for the area, but the gift was an early and disquieting sign that the board of managers would use the growing endowment for purposes that strayed from the original mission to educate orphan children.

After John Hershey's retirement in 1980 and Bill Fisher's in 1990, the composition of the board changed to include a number of outsiders with national reputations in education and child development. Over time, the four Hershey boards became interlocking. Many members served on multiple boards. It was a cozy setup, with potential for abuse. With access to virtually unlimited funds and virtually no one to answer to long after the demise of Mr. Hershey and his peers, the board began to institute changes that tinkered with the fundamental core values of the school.

Although the experience of growing up at Milton Hershey School demanded order, obedience, and compliant behavior, the perceived radical reform pushed the COWS out of their comfort zone. After more than ten years of frustration, the alumni finally blew its collective stack. This time, we would make a huge impact.

8

MELTDOWN IN CHOCOLATETOWN

A Hershey without chocolate? *The Harrisburg Patriot News*

The think-tank proposal known as CHILD stung the alumni. President Lepley's plan reportedly called for $25 million to establish the institute and a promise to never allow the institute's cost to exceed 50 percent of the school's operating budget. That would allow roughly $100 million per year to be diverted from the "Orphan Trust" today. Alumni felt this would be at odds with Mr. Hershey's intent. It would divert millions of dollars from needy children at a time when enrollment at Milton Hershey School hovered around one thousand, about the same number of students who were enrolled in 1937 and five hundred fewer than earlier enrollment peaks! It seemed obvious to graduates that the board was not living up to Mr. Hershey's deed of trust to care for more needy children even as the value of the trust skyrocketed to billions of dollars.

Moreover, the notion that Milton Hershey School could lecture anyone on the merits of quality education also rang hollow. At that time, the school's accreditation was being challenged, and despite all the efforts to turn our Home into an elite school for bright but underprivileged working-class kids, the school performed moderately at best.

Graduates were thrilled when the Dauphin County Orphan Court blocked the diversion of funds for the think tank. The Orphan Court, Pennsylvania's version of probate court, had played an important role in the past to modernize elements of the deed of trust, such as expanding enrollment to include girls and students of color. The court would become more involved in Milton Hershey School over the next few years.

As the twenty-first century began, the difference in perception between President Lepley and the current board versus the Alumni Association was as great as if we spoke different languages. They seemed to see Milton Hershey School as a special school for bright but disadvantaged kids. We viewed Milton Hershey School as a home and as a last resort for desperately poor kids who otherwise would fall through the cracks. The students the school officials wanted to enroll frequently belonged to intact families who did not have much money. The definition of "orphan" by now had been stretched past its limits. Many of these bright kids would do well in any setting. We saw the school as the one place where children from seriously dysfunctional environments could be saved, kids who had no other decent options.

Of course, the alumni views were not monolithic. I am among the first to acknowledge that some of my brothers resisted change of any sort. They wanted Milton Hershey School to remain frozen in time like a tintype image from another era. I strongly favored modernization, but I felt just as strongly that the core values articulated by Mr. Hershey in his deed of trust and practiced by him in his lifetime were enduring values that needed to be saved and, more important, could be saved. In some ways, I could understand both sides, although my emotions and loyalty put me firmly on the side of my fellow HomeGuys throughout the struggle.

There is considerable irony in the fact that my desire to bring Milton Hershey School into the modern age to best prepare our students for their future lives eventually caused an estrangement between me and a few militant colleagues. The history of any struggle shows that the most militant often win the battles and may even help to win the war. But they often can't survive the peace. They simply cannot or will not shift from the anger and fire of the firefight to the more mundane process of implementing incremental change and improvement. But at this critical juncture, the alumni were unified against a common enemy. Just as we observed the oath of silence and stuck up for one another as boys, we now stood shoulder to shoulder against authorities whom we felt were betraying Mr. Hershey's vision.

President Lepley and the board were not accustomed to being challenged. After Judge Morgan's ruling, the board of managers hired the firm of Kirkpatrick and Lockhart and former Pennsylvania governor Dick Thornburgh to conduct an "independent legal review" on the manner in which the board, the school, and the trustees were carrying out the provisions of the deed of trust. The act of commissioning this review reflected the board's discomfort with public criticism. The alumni deemed the review a whitewash. The report focused narrowly on the legality of the board's actions and never bothered to explore Mr. Hershey's "intent." To alumni leaders, this report was all about optics, just like that marketing study commissioned years earlier. Moreover, it was learned from newspaper accounts that Governor Thornburgh had a long and friendly association with President Lepley and had used Founder's Hall for his inaugural balls, so he was hardly "independent," in our eyes.

In response, the Alumni Association did its own exhaustive review of the history of the school and Mr. Hershey's intent. This report, "Bias, Flaw and Avoidance: A response to the Kirkpatrick and Lockhart Report," came out in October of 2000 and concluded that the board was acting in violation of Mr. Hershey's express desires.

Things were heating up.

The years of Milton Hershey School living in isolation at a far remove from the outside world were effectively over. The involvement of government officials and the courts and the role of the press began to act as a counterweight to the unquestioned power of the board of managers. The board never really lost its power, but for a few years it acknowledged the court of public opinion and responded to the concerns of its critics. This created a false sense of security and victory for the alumni because some of the politicians who were originally seen as saviors recognized a honey pot when they saw it in the "candy store" called the Milton Hershey Trust. There is considerable irony in the fact that "going public" did help to save the school and its soul but also created a new class of opportunists and a new set of problems for the future that last until this day.

The buildup of pressure from ten years of tension began to crack the walls of Milton Hershey School governance. The stress on the school was apparent. Houseparents mounted a public protest in 2000 on the lack of discipline and security in the student homes. This was a stunning event that provided concrete proof that the school culture was deteriorating. President Lepley had wanted to transform the school from a sprawling ten-thousand-acre campus into a centralized campus of about one thousand acres with a new town center. He oversaw a tremendous amount of construction as old student homes were sold or repurposed, beautiful Dutch barns were razed, and new homes were built on a smaller footprint. An experimental change also put children of vastly different ages into the same student homes. That made younger students potentially more vulnerable in the eyes of the Alumni Association.

For the grand opening of the centralized campus that year, about two hundred alumni showed up at Founder's Hall to bring the fight over the direction of Milton Hershey School onto school property for the first time. A newly hired director of security and a band of rent-a-cops met us and told us we were neither invited nor welcome. We were defiant. This was our home and we were Mr. Hershey's children. We had every right to be there. COWS had contacted the local media, and the TV stations were itching for a good story while the school administration was determined to keep us out. They erected chest-high snow fences around the entire town center. Alumni protestors were kept at bay but would not be denied. Our chants and colorful, handmade signs distracted the crowd and disrupted the ceremony. Finally, alumni were making their concerns known.

It is fair to say that the rabble-rousing by the Milton Hershey School Alumni Association attracted the notice of the media and that, in turn, attracted the notice of key public officials. Then as now, politicians are always assessing and sensitive to the state of public opinion. Our rag-tag band of orphan alumni in Chocolatetown and the debate over the future of the richest orphanage in the world proved to be an irresistible story for major news outlets from the *Philadelphia Inquirer* to the *New York Times* and then for *CBS News'* fabled Sunday-night magazine show, *60 Minutes*. The *60 Minutes* piece ran in December 2001. Alumni felt it was far too sympathetic to school officials, but the public exposure proved to be enormously helpful to our cause.

The Alumni Association had no legal standing apart from our ethical view of ourselves as the "children" and heirs of Milton Hershey, so it was crucial to get the government on our side. The first helpful politician to get involved was state attorney general D. Michael Fisher. Mike Fisher had been elected as the state's top law officer in 1996 and had then won reelection in 2000. A Republican, he was pegged as a major player by political reporters in Harrisburg. At the time, his ambitions and our cause were aligned. His involvement had already proved to be pivotal in stopping the diversion of money for the think tank.

The board gradually recognized that it was losing ground. The state attorney general issued a hard-hitting report within weeks of the *60 Minutes* piece. The report and a national news story delivered a one-two punch that put the board on defense. For the first time ever, the board agreed to engage in direct negotiations to find common ground with the alumni. The Office of the Attorney General established a panel for the negotiations, which included senior officials from the school, members of the attorney general's staff as well as two officers from the Alumni Association: a former administrator and me. This was big. This was the first time in school history that alumni leaders had been invited to the policy round-table.

Negotiations went on for nearly a year. The alumni had gathered so much data about school enrollment practices, student safety issues, and collapsing employee morale that we made major headway. When the school officials attempted to defend their track record, we simply presented their own data, which showed the enrollment of less-needy children, higher attrition rates, soaring budgets without any growth in enrollment, and serious security breaches. Milton Hershey School staff on the inside funneled accurate data to us. Shockingly, the students and graduates were being heard by someone who could actually make a difference. Even the omnipotent board of managers was accountable to the Charitable Trust Division of the attorney general's office. COWS were making real progress.

While the panel debated the operation and future of Milton Hershey School, the attorney general's office kept investigating the internal financial structure and behavior of the trust board. The attorney general had jurisdiction over charities and trusts, and the endowment had grown into billions of dollars. The *Philadelphia Inquirer* reported that a deputy attorney general told the board that the Milton Hershey School Trust was dangerously exposed because most of the assets were tied up in the Hershey companies. With the shocking collapse of Enron and WorldCom in the news at that time, the sound practice of portfolio diversification became an essential best practice for all investment funds. Heaven forbid there should be a worldwide sugar shortage or cocoa bean blight! Almost half of the school's trust could be wiped out swiftly, so reliant was the board upon Hershey stock. The attorney general's office raised critical issues about the fiduciary responsibility of the trustees.

While it was true that the school's fortunes rose and fell with the fate of the Hershey Company, there was no indication that the American public would grow weary of chocolate candy. The community was also one with the chocolate factory. The town of Hershey had been built from scratch around that factory. The very name of the town was the same as its founder. So it was hard to even imagine Hershey, Pennsylvania, without a huge candy factory and the chocolate company headquarters.

However, the Milton Hershey School Trust Board, likely feeling beleaguered from the ongoing criticism and queasy about getting on the wrong side of the state's top law-enforcement official, decided they needed to put the company up for sale. It was not wholly irrational. The trustees had a responsibility to the school and reasonable people could debate the prudence of diversifying the Milton Hershey School endowment. Years earlier, Mr. Hershey himself had considered selling the company. Mr. Hershey's plan to sell his chocolate company for $50 million to help fund the school's expansion in 1929 was dashed by the onset of Black Friday and the Great Depression. The board, keeping with its practice, made the decision to sell in total secrecy.

The Milton Hershey School Trust Board initially put out a confidential search for buyers in the spring of 2002. There was a lot of interest. The Hershey companies were profitable and solid, so the major food conglomerates, including Kraft and Nestle, were very interested. The William Wrigley Company, producer of the famous chewing gum, that was founded by a contemporary and rival of Milton Hershey, eventually offered a stunning $12.5 billion. The secret could not keep forever. Dozens of analysts, lawyers, and corporate executives knew about the availability of the company. The *Wall Street Journal* broke the story of the Wrigley offer on July 25, 2001, and all hell broke loose in Chocolatetown.

There had always been tension between the town of Hershey and our school. Despite the widespread knowledge that the company existed largely to serve Milton Hershey School, even the employees kept a distance from school issues. Those of us who grew up at the school felt that some townspeople looked down on us. Few of us ever entered a private home in the town. The few of us who did, like me, were invited to one of our teacher's homes. There were some townies who resented that Mr. Hershey had left most of his wealth to these poor, out-of-town, troubled youth who bore little resemblance to their own well-behaved children who attended the fine local public schools. Others thought that Milton Hershey School graduates should be more grateful for all we had been given and not bite the hand that had fed us.

Few people in the town stayed up at night worrying about our school, but the Hershey companies were central to the economic life of the community as well as its very identity. The prospect of a sale fired up the town, and a raucous "Derail the Sale" campaign was mounted. It did not take much imagination to see the implications of a sale to a big company with no ties to the Hershey community. Everyone who worked at the company or relied upon the company for business or just lived in a town where the scent of chocolate was ever-present in the air felt threatened. We had different agendas: the Milton Hershey School alumni were concerned about the school, and the town was worried about the chocolate factory. But we all were questioning the judgment of the board. So this time, the orphans and the town came together as one. At long last, the good residents of Hershey and the thousands of employees of the Hershey Chocolate Company joined us on the ramparts.

By now Attorney General Mike Fisher was running for governor of Pennsylvania against Ed Rendell, chairman of the Democratic National Committee and former mayor of Philadelphia. Although his own deputy had lit the fuse by suggesting the trust diversify its holdings to honor its fiduciary responsibilities to the school, Fisher did an amazing reversal of his position and went to court to prevent the sale. He never did address his apparent switch of position, but politicians are practical people. A strong majority of Pennsylvania voters opposed the sale of the iconic Hershey Company to a multinational, out-of-state food conglomerate. Let's see. Diversify, which is a sound move for the Milton Hershey School Trust, or get more votes? The potential sale so unnerved the state that the attorney general and the state legislature actually developed tough new restrictions to make it harder to sell some corporations headquartered in Pennsylvania.

The Milton Hershey School Board called an emergency meeting and voted to take the company off the auction block. Close friends who worked at major Wall Street brokerage firms had mocked my belief that the sales process could be reversed. Virtually every corporation that received attractive offers once it was in play had been sold in the past. That was true until this case. We were all amazed by the speed of the reversal.

Mike Fisher lost the election that November, but his office finished up the work of the year-long Milton Hershey School negotiations with a formal recommendation later that month to the board of managers. By now, the board seemed really rattled. The official directives were compiled in a historic document, "The Office of the Attorney General–Milton Hershey School Agreements of 2002." The first agreement called for reform of board-membership criteria to minimize conflicts of interest and curb the practice of a few individuals controlling the interlocking interests of the various Hershey entities. The second specified student-enrollment criteria based upon financial need, IQ, and social need to make certain that the school would again serve the neediest kids. It also said that every student had the right and should have access to complete services 365 days a year, emphasizing alumni insistence that the school be a home not just a school. In my mind, this was the most important document in Milton Hershey School history since the deed of trust itself. Sadly, it would not stand for even a single year.

After so many years of fighting, graduates could finally exhale. While we did not get everything we wanted, these critical reforms guaranteed that our beloved school would once again become a home to and save the lives of kids like us. And a step had been taken to curtail the absolute power of the Milton Hershey School Trust Board. The Spartans had won!

President William Lepley had announced his intent to retire in a year the previous June. Most alumni welcomed the change of command. It was time for new leadership. We could hope that the next president would be more sympathetic to alumni concerns and would strengthen the traditional values of discipline, hard work, and accountability at to our school.

The pieces began to fall into place like parts of a puzzle. On November 15, 2002, the board of managers was reorganized at the implicit direction of the attorney general and the Orphan's Court. The ten directors viewed as most supportive of the sale of the Hershey companies were asked to resign, including Dr. Lepley, who tendered his formal resignation, effective at the end of the month.

On November 16, 2002, the new board was announced by the attorney general. The new trust board included the six members who had voted at least once against selling the company and added four new members handpicked by the Office of the Attorney General with input from the Orphan's Court and a few retired board members. One of these new members was former attorney general Leroy S. Zimmerman, one of the most powerful Republicans in the state. Zimmerman, a senior partner at a Harrisburg law firm, was the first elected attorney general of Pennsylvania. Another was the former president of the *Harrisburg Patriot News.* I welcomed their appointment. I did not see that a powerful politician and a man with inordinate influence over local media could potentially deprive the alumni of two key avenues for redress.

With President Lepley departing, Milton Hershey School would be without a leader in a matter of weeks. It had taken the school as long as a year to recruit its prior presidents. The alumni and the reconstituted board were worried about the effect of a leadership vacuum on the operation of the school. Milton Hershey School was becoming chaotic because of the disarray at the top, the policies that had eroded the old culture, and the demoralized staff. The alumni assumed that the board would make an interim appointment from the current administrative team even though most senior officials were tainted by their association with the former regime.

The dramatic reconstitution of the board, the president's departure, and the formal vote to stop the sale shocked me to the core. It was stunning to see so much change in a single day when change had been glacial in the past. More governance reform had occurred in two weeks than in the past ninety years. I was not prepared for what came next.

I was working at my office at Renaissance Leadership on the Chesapeake Bay when my administrative assistant notified me that one of the six surviving board members was on the phone for me. I took a deep breath before picking up the phone. No board member had ever reached out to me before. I will never forget what he said.

The board member, an alumnus, said that the school needed an interim president, and several credible sources recommended I be consulted. This did not surprise me. I had strong allies among the alumni, staff, and former board members who would want me to be consulted for input into this decision. My views might be helpful, and I certainly would welcome the chance to contribute any expertise I might have to our school.

But then he said something very odd.

"We need someone who can fill the job in two weeks. I assume you can't break away from your business that quickly."

I was confused. What was he saying? I hesitated for a moment, trying to compute the meaning behind his words.

"Are you asking me to be a serious candidate for the MHS presidency?"

He did not pause. "Yes," he said, and then stated that there would only be a few candidates, it had to be quick, and that was why they assumed I was not likely to be available.

The smartass in me was dying to ask him if this was some new-fangled recruitment strategy: tell a prospective candidate that he is probably not available. It was a peculiar way to ask if I was interested in the job.

I focused on the process and asked about the timeline for selection. He said that several board members would interview candidates by phone over the next two days and then make a decision by the end of the week. He then added, again, something about understanding if I was not interested or available.

Suddenly, a deep and clear force within me took charge. Everything that had led to this point came together with quiet clarity: the terrified three year old cradled in Pop Arbogast's arms; the powerless twelve year old who watched his brother go mad; the sixteen year old who led our Spartans to victory on the gridiron; the fifty-nine year old with a lifetime of attachment to his old Home. I was being called to service.

I wrote down my response in my journal after that call: "I will be up there tomorrow if the board will have me. Our Home is off mission and students are at risk. There is no greater priority in my life."

After hanging up the telephone, I sat motionless at my desk for a long time to process what had just happened. I was being recruited to lead Milton Hershey School; I was being asked to come Home again; and uh oh, I agreed to be considered for the job without first talking it over with my wife Gail.

The last point troubled me. Gail and I were partners. We discussed all major decisions in our lives and made those decisions together. How in the world could I say I might move back to Hershey and take a new job without talking to her? Gail did understand the depth of my passion and connection to the school. More like an obsession, she remarked. I also had to figure out what I would do about my business if I was selected. The company had a dozen big clients and as many employees who depended upon me. In addition, Gail and I were just months away from completing construction of our dream home on the eastern shore of the Chesapeake Bay. We had been working on the house for the past eighteen months.

We talked it through. Gail knew what this meant to me. And a great partner never gets in the way of a rare, true calling. We worked it out. We agreed that if I was offered the interim job, I would go to Hershey and she would stay in Maryland to finish our new home. I would drive back to the Eastern Shore on most weekends and she would drive up to Milton Hershey School for big events. If I became permanent president, we would revisit the arrangement.

Two of the surviving board members subsequently interviewed me by phone for barely an hour. They were most concerned with how I would handle an interim role and what I would do to raise employee morale at the school.

One startled me again when he asked if I was interested in holding the presidency on a permanent basis. I was. I was not about to undertake the most important challenge of my life and not complete it if I could do so. In that case, he said, I might want to pass on being the interim leader. He warned me that the school was in such turmoil that the interim president would have a hard time performing well in that tough environment.

I told him that I could not sit there polishing my resume while my Home and the kids were in trouble. The very next day, I got the job offer. Wow! I was shocked and delighted and honored beyond belief. I had resigned myself to never getting inside the big tent after taking a leadership role in the dissent. After all this time, I never dreamed I would get a chance to lead the most remarkable school on earth. I would be in a position to help restore Milton and Catherine Hershey's mission and save the lives of many more children. Wow!

On November 19, 2002, my interim role was announced. On November 30, President Lepley formally resigned. On December 1, I started work as interim president. I was home again. This time with a sacred assignment.

9

THE RESTORATION OF MR. HERSHEY'S VISION

Our kids help rededicate Old Senior Hall as Catherine Hall, 2007. *Courtesy of the Milton Hershey School*

When I returned to Milton Hershey School to be its interim president, my mind and heart were exploding with Spartan pride and possibilities. Gail and I drove slowly through the campus, absorbing the sights and sounds of arguably the most remarkable private school in the world. In my reverie, I sensed hundreds of amazing kids and their houseparents going through the bedtime rituals before lights out just as Frankie and I had with Pop Arbogast. Gail nudged me back to reality and teasingly noted that "this time I would have to stay and deliver the goods." When I feigned ignorance, she pointed out that I could pontificate about high performance for three days at my Renaissance executive seminars and then fly home to the Bay and my dog. Not this time. I chuckled at and cherished her unvarnished candor.

From day one, it was apparent that the morale of students and staff had fallen lower than the old manure pits at the dairy barns. School assemblies were muted and passive. The cocurricular activities were lightly attended. Apathy was the new normal. So I turned myself into the cheerleader in chief. When a local news reporter asked me if I would use the CEO title as some of my predecessors had, I replied, "Never! Unless you mean Chief Encouragement Officer!" Change is never easy, and I threw myself completely into the task of persuading both adults and students to experience the school in a different way.

My life journey informed my tenure at Milton Hershey School. The terrified three year old who arrived at Hershey Industrial School after World War II was still a part of me. But I was also a mature man who had a lifetime of experiences, a terrific education, and a deep knowledge about what made success. Somehow I had to bring all those things together. On day one, I retraced some of the steps of my childhood and youth. I returned to my grade-school cottage, Caaba. I remembered the loving support Frankie and I received from Mom and Pop Arbogast. Their nurture planted a seed of hope and worthiness in our hearts. I knelt at the base of the same pine tree where we had set up our little plastic army soldiers to fight our version of the Korean War. Eddie and I had engaged in massive assaults on one another's soldiers while Frankie characteristically hung back with his Red Cross ambulance to rescue the wounded. So much time had passed; both the tree and I had tripled in size since those days.

I drove over the hill to Spring Creek (Unit Number 34) and remembered the seven-days-a-week labor involved in running a large dairy farm. Hard work and play in a common cause and delayed gratification were all key virtues baked into the typical HomeGuy. Character development was essential to the Milton Hershey School mission. It was more important than chemistry or algebra. The strength of character to do the right thing, to persevere during tough times, and to be "good citizens," in the words of Milton Hershey, were all crucial. I understood this truth because I had lived it. I knew in my bones the difference between a houseparent who was going through the motions, just doing his job, and an adult who sincerely cared about the child. I did not want staff on power trips, playing favorites, or punishing a kid just because he looked at a houseparent "the wrong way." We would be tough and direct in response to inappropriate student behavior, but consequences had to be fair and come from truly caring adults who would love and discipline our kids with equal intensity.

For our game plan, I teased out the fundamental values that allowed generations of orphans to survive and thrive at the school: hard work, perseverance, self-discipline. Then I added the profiles of great corporate leaders I had supported during thirty years of high-performance coaching. It should be no surprise that those enlightened principles were modeled by Milton Hershey himself. They were humility, vision, generosity, courage, and a mighty work ethic.

I also applied the profile I had used for years in corporate coaching to the history of Milton Hershey School management practices. The school had once excelled at encouraging hard work, self-sacrifice, and commitment to the greater good, but recently it had declined in those qualities. There were other characteristics that Mr. Hershey possessed—vision, the courage to experiment and innovate, and the willingness to change when warranted—that had rarely been seen at the school. The century-long custodial mindset at Milton Hershey School viewed innovation as an unnecessary risk. This could not stand. Milton Hershey School could choose to be safe, predictable, and in control through a regimented, uniform program, but the school, its staff, and students would never reach full potential without taking a few chances and embracing thoughtful change to make things better. Somehow, we needed to build the courage to risk significant change if our students were to enjoy success beyond the Spartan bubble.

I hit the ground running from the start and bet everything on a policy of full engagement and transparency. Every day I met with a half dozen groups: teachers, houseparents, students, administrators, and support staff, both separately and together. I named an independent Discovery Team of highly respected alumni, recent retirees, and several boarding-school experts to dig down and learn deeply and honestly about the people and the practices of Milton Hershey School today. We needed an accurate reality check on which to base our reform.

After all those years of coaching clients, I followed the advice I had given executives countless times: I spoke the truth as I knew it; I listened with my heart; and I dreamed big with clear intention. I was cautioned that I likely would never get the job permanently if I rocked the boat too much. But I was not constitutionally capable of being a cautious caretaker.

To me, the Milton Hershey School boat had run aground and was taking on water like a damaged sailboat on a rocky shoal on Chesapeake Bay. If the school was to become better, safer, and more aligned with Mr. Hershey's vision, then I would have to rock the boat fairly hard. On January 14, 2003, I restructured the administration of the school into a new Leadership Team with twelve members. The change was disruptive for the school and for individuals, but I needed a team with members who would all row in the same direction with the same intensity. Some people left. New people were hired who shared the Spartan vision. Among the key hires to the new Leadership Team were five highly successful alumni. Three had an inordinate impact on the resurgence of Milton Hershey School. Bob Fehrs, Class of '63, head of the Middle Division, oversaw the $100 million restoration of Old Senior Hall and built a strong and proud Middle Division on a new campus. Pete Gurt, Class of '85, who rose to become vice president of student life, was my right-hand man and a very effective leader of school operations. Nick Nissley, Class of '84 and vice president of human resources and professional development, became my invaluable partner in culture change. He was also the lead architect of our emerging strategic plan.

I never pulled a punch. When I was interviewed for our school bulletin, I revisited happy memories from the past and spoke about my favorite teacher and even my favorite food at Hershey Industrial School: Shepherd's pie and apple dumpling. I spoke frankly about envisioned changes. Then the interviewer caught me by surprise, asking, "What do you want to be called?"

It was not an idle question. My first thoughts went back to the houseparents who refused to call me by my preferred name. So I said, "Johnny."

She followed up, "Well, OK, so the staff can call you Johnny. What do you want the students to call you?"

I mumbled some words to buy time to think. I do not like titles. I feel that many times titles are used to create distance and puff up the prestige of the self-important. I did not want to be called Mr. O'Brien or President O'Brien. So I blurted out, "Johnny O." The interviewer said, "Wow!"

Then a few members of my Leadership Team said, "Whoa!" worried that I would be encouraging disrespect and too much familiarity with a nickname. Our communications director urged me to reconsider and change my answer before the school bulletin was published. I thought hard about it overnight and decided I did not want to use a formal title to induce respect. The job itself came with so much power that I would rather earn respect from the students than demand it. And at the end of the day, I did not want to be called something that did not suit me. Being a fairly informal and friendly guy, "Johnny O." worked for me.

Management experts might disagree with me, but "Johnny O." reduced the enormous chasm between the exalted authority figures of Milton Hershey School and our students, the true beneficiaries of the school. To be sure, a few students exploited the opportunity to disrespect their president in public. But when posed with these challenges to authority, I like to think I was able to turn the disrespect into a teachable moment about the importance of respect freely given.

I structured my schedule to spend as much time with the students as I spent with the staff. I was in their faces all the time: on the playing fields, at theater and music practice, at Student Council meetings, and at their student homes for dinner. I was ever-present; asking questions, listening intently, dreaming, and encouraging them every step of the way. Gradually, the students began to realize that I cared deeply about their success. This was purely personal to me. They knew I had walked in their school-issued shoes, sat in their seats, and lived the life of an orphan.

I began every assembly and worship service by saying, "This is the day that the Lord hath made" until students and adults responded with "Let us rejoice and be glad in it." Then I would cite several specific examples of how fortunate we were at Milton Hershey School on that day. Counting out loud the blessings of ample resources, a noble mission, and a dedicated staff over and over was thought to be hokey and a bit too rah-rah by some until it became contagious and started evolving into "the way we think around here." People who deeply appreciate their blessings begin acting that way.

My highest priority was providing a safe and nurturing environment for emotionally scarred children. The systematic bullying of my school days was long gone, but abuse and disrespect still took place in more random and subtle ways. The change reflected the historic changes in the student body and society. The student body had been transformed from that of all white boys of my era to a rainbow of black, Hispanic, white, and Asian children—half of them girls. The fastest growing category of Spartans was "other/mixed" students whose very existence and mixed racial background personified diversity, just as the first mixed-race president of the United States would a few years later.

As someone who had grown up in a society still segregated by practice and sometimes by law, I was amazed by the incredible and lasting friendships untouched by old racial barriers. In our grade-school homes, the children were totally colorblind! They simply did not see housemates and friends of different colors and races as different from them in any way. Their experience showed that racism, like a lot of other evils, is something children learn. That is not to say that there was no friction. When you put children from disadvantaged backgrounds into the same big melting pot, there is tension and conflict. We worked hard to sort out the good-natured, bustin', natural growing pains and the letting-off-steam from intentional harm. Then we dealt with abuse immediately.

I met with each bully personally. It was one offense that automatically caused the culprit to be sent to the president's office. "Mutual respect" was a sacred value, and we worked consciously to replace abusive behavior with active respect. Benign neglect or even the absence of bullying was not enough in my view. Being ignored can be as brutally damaging a fate for a child as being abused by a bully. We strove for the lofty ideal of "actively valuing one another for our differences." To do that requires deep self-respect, so we focused first on building that. Some on my team teased me for hugging a bully on the way out of my office, but bullies lash out to gain respect they don't have. Their broken hearts need treatment too.

In that spirit, I established the Spartan Peace Prize and made it the highest award a Spartan student could earn. It was presented on Dr. Martin Luther King's birthday in January to the high-school student who did the most to promote respect and who actively championed the cause of the smaller, weaker, newer, and different students who were most vulnerable to abuse. It was named for Frankie O'Brien, Class of '59, and it became the most coveted prize for our student body.

The many demands involved in running a year-round program on a ten-thousand-plus-acre campus with even more staff than students would make it easy to lose sight of the sole purpose of Milton Hershey School: student success. So being with the students was my highest priority. The kids were refreshingly candid, and it did not take long to discover that the student body suffered from the same crippling ailment as the workforce: entitlement syndrome. This is a constant danger for an institution of such extraordinary wealth. A pervasive sense of entitlement was not an issue when the school had a smaller endowment and operated on Mr. Hershey's strong belief in frugality and an abhorrence of waste. But the spigots cranked wide open with the 21st Century Initiative when the budget doubled within five years even as fewer students were served.

When I initially asked students to name the greatest benefit of Milton Hershey School, every single one replied, "the college scholarship." Policy changes in the past decade had granted every graduating senior unlimited financial aid to whatever college that would take them. Campus doors flung wide open. Almost any college was eager to accept disadvantaged and minority-group students who were bringing full tuition payments with them! When I pressed the students to identify a way the school had benefited their lives now, not in the future, they struggled for an answer. A few students said sports. One said, "Driver's Ed." Most reverted to the college scholarship answer.

Helping our students to continue their postsecondary study was a good thing. Most parents with means provide that opportunity to their children, and the workforce demands of the twenty-first century required students to have some skill, expertise, or higher level of education than high school. But students could not take this opportunity for granted if they were to really appreciate it. They needed to earn it. We immediately began to overhaul the college scholarship program to require students to earn their financial aid through achievement and behavior starting in the ninth grade. There would be consequences, both good and bad, for everyday behavior and performance. No longer would the school pay for a graduate to go to the University of Hawaii for a nursing degree just because his or her best friend was going there when one of the country's best nursing programs was located two miles away in Hershey at one-fourth the cost. The remedy for both students and adults was to ask more of them and shower them with less.

One of the first expenditures I approved was for lawn mowers for each student home. Chores are an essential building block to character development, a work ethic, and discipline. It struck me as profoundly wrong that the school staff cut the grass while the students lounged inside on a couch playing video games. That changed. We immediately restricted personal laptop computers to juniors and seniors when reports showed that ninth and tenth graders were trashing, losing, or selling an alarming number of personal computers. A half-dozen desktop computers were already in each student home and more were put in most classrooms so there would be no shortage of computer education or access. We recognized the value of the computer as a teaching and learning tool. And we reinstituted the restitution program. If students lost or flagrantly damaged a piece of property, they would work at the school to pay for it. This is something a good parent would do. Accountability and an appreciative spirit came roaring back.

The students responded like a neglected garden to a gush of water after a lengthy drought. Growing children want to be challenged. By our asking more from them, they discovered they had more to offer than they realized. By our being honest with them and giving them less stuff, our children developed a greater appreciation for what they had and, more important, they realized we genuinely cared about them and their welfare. Children need boundaries and rules to make them feel safe just as they need opportunities to experiment and grow. We worked hard to strike a balance.

After six weeks of work, the Discovery Team reported its findings to me. We shocked folks by presenting the findings verbatim to the school community. I wanted the community to see everything I saw, unvarnished, and to embrace these recommendations as I did. We then hashed out with our board a clear, bold, and unequivocal vision for Milton Hershey School.

1. We would return to the Milton Hershey School mission of serving children with high financial and social need, those vulnerable children with the fewest adults in their lives.

2. We would serve our children as a year-round home again.
3. We would expand enrollment (then at about 1,200) to serve at least 2,000 children no later than 2013.

I thought long and hard about how to present this new message to the troops who would be responsible for implementing the vision. Rather than sending them another document, I took it to them in a series of all-day workshops on the school's future called "Onward Spartans," which I facilitated personally. To get to the mountaintop, we needed to rebuild trust and pride and do it quickly. I knew from experience that it is easy to set lofty goals but really hard to gain ownership of those outcomes and agree on how to reach them. The process involves deep engagement, genuine debate, listening, and vulnerability, especially for the leader. So we played, debated, laughed, and even cried together during those sessions and hammered out a consensus on the core values and behaviors that had to be made sacred if we were to create a better Milton Hershey School. We came up with four sacred values and the essential behavior required to revive the Spartan culture. We called it the Milton Hershey Way.

INTEGRITY

Speaks openly and honestly and does not gossip.

POSITIVE SPIRIT

Shows up enthusiastically with a can-do attitude toward work and school.

COMMITMENT TO MISSION

Puts the school and our mission above own personal interests.

MUTUAL RESPECT

Actively respects and assumes the best in everyone.

Nothing was novel about these principles. They were broadly similar to the core values adopted by hundreds of organizations I had coached. In fact, the specific choice of words mattered little. What mattered was commitment to those values. So we hired, promoted, and fired based upon our sacred values. We began every weekly Leadership Team meeting with examples of being on or off our sacred values. All manager appraisals included feedback on employee behavior based on the sacred values. We turned our values into "the way we do things around here." We kept that up every week for more than six years until the principles gradually became the norm and set the expectation.

Shifting back to the 24-7 year-round model and being *in loco paren-tis* all the time was one of the toughest adjustments for the staff and students. We shortened the summer by adding four weeks to the school year and launched a fun, exciting, summer-learning program to serve the children who could not and probably should not return to what they still viewed as home for any significant length of time. Teachers and houseparents told me how the children who returned to severely disad-vantaged homes for the entire summer seriously regressed. They forgot their manners, stopped doing chores, and lost so much progress from the previous year that September was like ground hog day, a complete do-over of the prior year. Some, to our horror, got involved with drugs and even brought them back to campus.

A number of the parents and sponsors who had enrolled their chil-dren in a "fine boarding school" balked at our return to Mr. Hershey's mission. A few withdrew their kids. We expected that. Milton Hershey was not going to be a way station to a free education for intact families of modest means any longer. We also expected the students to rebel against the longer school year and shorter vacations. My Leadership Team and I repeatedly explained the absolute necessity of returning the school to our founder's mission. Some of the students did not like it, or me, very much at first. But they started to understand. They did like the signs on my desk and conference table that read "QUESTION AU-THORITY . . . Respectfully." I added "Respectfully" after my first month of student meetings. I had grown up in this school where we were taught to respect and, especially, fear authority. Now, we favored questioning and learning over positional power.

The Leadership Team then recommended we eliminate a popular treat, Hershey Park Day, an annual day off school to go to Hershey Park. Even I thought that might be going too far. "We can't take Her-shey Park Day away from them when they are rioting about having to stay here year-round," I protested.

Our savvy high-school principal, Jack Storm, said of course we could. The students could already go to Hershey Park for free every weekend. Why, he asked, should we lose a whole day of school and pay $70,000 for one more play day?

He was right and I was wrong. By our eliminating Hershey Park Day, student attention shifted away from the loss of their three-month summer vacation to "Save Hershey Park Day" rallies. It was a classic bait-and-switch tactic to divert attention. Jack shrewdly pointed out that students have a short-term focus; they care about today. A few *might* think about the week to come. In any case, the students were far more resilient than the adult staff and quickly adapted to the new normal.

I zeroed in on the Milton Hershey School Marching Band as one place to make a breakthrough on morale. What better speaks to a high school's spirit than its year-round marching band? Our Spartan band had lost much of its spirit, pride, and numbers, and it had declined in physical appearance. I winced a bit when our marching band ambled into Spartan stadium—and even more so when the glorious bands of our opponents performed at halftime.

It did not take much to turn it around. We empowered the band director, communicated a higher level of expectations, promoted the band at assemblies, and bought them spiffy new uniforms. A transformation began to take place. By the second year, the band members and a few staff noticed the improvement. By the third year, the entire student body and school community stood a bit taller when the Spartan Band marched in their presence. State and regional awards for performance followed. I cannot say that the band's improvement led directly to the success of our sports teams, which suddenly got into playoffs more often, but the band unquestionably trumpeted a turnaround message: Milton Hershey School is back with pride and excellence.

I made a point of personally greeting our marching band when they strutted onto Spartan Field. I would shout out, "Greatest band in the land!" barely heard over their thumping rendition of "Onward Spartans." Their rousing performance never failed to give me goose bumps and a swell of pride. Everyone on campus took notice. Being a passionate athlete, I naturally attended the practices and games of our fierce football teams, but I grew especially close to our wrestlers and field-hockey girls as well. And to me, Spartan theater, music, and dance were just as precious.

I taught a class, "Being a Leader," and led a daylong outdoor leadership challenge for the incoming senior class. However, my most meaningful engagements with our students were the spontaneous ones. A few took place in our Agricultural and Environmental Education (AEE) domain, the modern version of the dairy and farm work of my day. Just like then, a lot of our adolescents found comfort in being with animals on our magnificent agrarian campus. Animals don't talk back or judge or annoy. They just are. Many of our kids came from harsh city ghettoes without a bit of the green and the respite that nature provides. So animals, even crickets, scared many of them at first. But eventually, the cool green of our campus and the warmth of the farm animals gave them a bit of peace in which to deal with the turmoil of adolescence.

The first time I visited our AEE cow and goat barn, one of the few old Dutch barns still in use, I was greeted by two eighth-grade girls who could not contain their glee over a personal visit by the president. They eagerly introduced me to their prize goats that would be competing in an upcoming State Farm Show in Harrisburg. The girls, barely teenagers, described in detail the care and feeding of their goats and how this scrupulous attention might produce ribbons at the farm show. So far, few students had exhibited more passion and investment in a specific goal. I praised them and thanked them for their eye-opening goat tutorial. Explaining that I was "more of a cow expert myself," I told them a bit about my own adventures as a Milton Hershey School barnguy.

Bubbling with excitement, the girls exclaimed, "Well, you gotta see this, Johnny O.!" and pulled me over to a stall holding a single large Holstein. I thought to myself, "What's the big deal about a single cow?" They almost read my mind and pointed to a clear plastic disk about the size of a salad plate on the cow's side.

"See, Rumi has a big hole in her side so we can watch the digestive process of a dairy cow!" I figured it was a trick, like the ones played on me at my first Milton Hershey School milking so many years ago.

One of the girls leaned over to unscrew the plastic disk, revealing a gaping hole in the cow's side. I was horrified and urged her to put the disk back in place before the cow caught some infection and died.

One of the girls patted my hand. "It's OK. Look, we get to see into Rumi's rumen. That is how she got her name and we can watch her digest her hay." I edged closer and sure enough, I could see what looked like wet hay swirling around like dirty socks in an old washing machine.

I was still worried that Rumi might catch something, but the girls reassured me and explained that cows had four stomachs and were always digesting their food. That is why they were constantly chewing even when not eating.

I was truly amazed. After more than four thousand milkings, I had no idea how a cow's digestive system worked. Driving back to my office,

I realized these two eighth-grade girls had learned more about Holsteins in a few months of their AEE program than I had learned in years of "udder ignorance."

Weeks later, I went to our horse barn and expected to be amazed again because I knew about the therapeutic value of riding for children with emotional challenges. I still was not prepared for how adept our staff was at producing breakthroughs in some of the most vulnerable children. I watched a new student who had come to us from the coal-country city of Hazelton, Pennsylvania, approach a horse for the first time. The student was visibly trembling and did not look as though she would ever get close enough to the chestnut mare to put a bridle on her. The instructor whispered that this had been her third try that week. She sidled over to the student and said something encouraging. The student finally took the final two tentative steps to get within reach of the horse and after a lifetime pause lifted her trembling arm to the mare's neck and held it there for over ten seconds. I still have a vivid mental picture of that child overcoming her fear with the help of two kind teachers. It encapsulated everything we were trying to do for our HomeGuys and HomeGals.

For all our staff's miracles, we still had a big problem with student retention. We were losing more than 10 percent of our students each year. Leaving one's real home, even a dysfunctional one, is very difficult. As Frankie and I had, kids missed their mothers, siblings, and friends or just felt homesick for the familiar. Others had a difficult time following the rules and policies of the school. Most of the dropouts departed during the first year. It was wrenching to think about these kids returning to their bleak old lives, having lost probably the one opportunity they would ever have to escape a life of deprivation. Everyone decried our attrition problem, but the school had become resigned to it. "We have lost roughly the same percentage of kids for the last few decades" was how it was phrased. I said we had to take it head on. Hundreds of kids depended on it.

A special innovation team I commissioned developed something called "Springboard Academy," a separate school within the school to prepare new students for the Milton Hershey School Way for up to nine months before integrating them into the full program. For the first time in Milton Hershey School history, all children were not being treated exactly the same. Same was easy and safe. Same allows for more control and fewer problems, but same rarely improves anything. Springboard Academy was strongly opposed by some alumni and entrenched staff who viewed the dormitory-style rooms as a reversion to the earliest years of Hershey Industrial School or as a threat to their job security. But I was convinced that a friendly, summer-camp-type approach with more caregivers was exactly what was needed to help these students adjust to a world as different to them as a foreign country. We could finally learn better ways to deal with sponsoring families and homesickness.

We started the experiment with grades six and seven and then changed it to serve only eighth graders. It was expensive. It cost us $9,300 more per student per year, and we spent millions on a new campus. After three years, my successor ended the program because the program outcomes allegedly were not any better than the core program. But that was never the purpose of Springboard Academy. The purpose was to figure out how to better transition and retain more students.

Springboard needed at least four or five years to demonstrate its value, but by then I had no say in the matter. I will always be convinced it was a worthy experiment and eventually might have incredibly improved more kids' lives. In any case, trying and failing is preferable to accepting a 12 percent attrition rate as normal and doing nothing to provide an extra-hand-up to more than 150 children who return to poverty each year. An analogy would be to the federal Head Start program, which targets preschool poor children for extra enrichment. The early investment in these children often cannot be recognized for years, but that does not diminish the need and value.

Another long-term, troublesome problem was helping our students succeed after graduation. Legally, our responsibility ended on graduation day. But morally, these were our children. A parent would not toss their own eighteen-year-old son or daughter into the harsh reality of today's world the moment after their graduation from high school. Plenty of our students were street smart, but the school did not prepare them for the nitty gritty of everyday life post–high school. Milton Hershey School students still went from a dictated schedule and complete regimentation right up until graduation day and then off to total freedom the second they received their diplomas. In that sense, nothing had changed since I graduated.

Our students got $100 in cash, a diploma, and a suitcase of clothing and then vanished. We had never done a good job of systematically tracking the progress of our graduates. The school had some contact with those who enrolled in college because we sent checks to their colleges each semester. But we did not always know if the students were still enrolled or how well they were doing. The best assessment our school could come up with was that while roughly 90 percent of our graduates enrolled in college, around 35 percent graduated within five years. It was painfully apparent that a lot of kids stumbled, floundered, and flopped after leaving Milton Hershey School. It had nothing to do with innate ability or even desire. Without the support, regulations, and rigid structure of the institution, many young graduates simply did not know what to do.

If Milton Hershey School was to do its job properly, consistent with the terms of the deed of trust, we had to figure out a way to prepare our students better for postgraduate life. And if we were truly *in loco parentis*, we needed to develop a way to track our graduates and provide a helping hand to them as they made their way as fledgling adults. We launched a serious, longitudinal study on graduates, the first of its kind for Milton Hershey School, just to get some hard data on what happened to them and why upon leaving the Spartan bubble. And we simultaneously created a major counseling and outreach program to support our young alumni while they were in college or working in their first jobs. Eventually we created a young-alumni support program that provided a safety net for our graduates through their mid-twenties with counseling services, temporary housing, summer jobs, and the type of gentle safety net that all good parents provide for their emerging adults.

We also changed the school structure for our seniors. It was way past time to trust our oldest students and give them some practice at making plans and choices before the harsh reality of flying solo smacked them in the face. Our fledglings needed to learn the basics, from how to do their laundry and cook a simple meal, and how to open a checking account and pay a bill on time, to how get to an early-morning class without being roused by a houseparent. Too few of our eighteen-year-old graduates had family or advocates to support them after graduation, so we announced we would design and launch an independent-living program for seniors.

The very week I asked for proposals, I was stunned when three different plans landed on my desk. They dated back as far as the 1980s. I should not have been surprised that Milton Hershey School leaders had always known that some form of transitional living experience was needed to help graduates succeed, but no one had been willing to pull the trigger. I understood the self-serving reluctance. Giving 200 seventeen year olds freedom to determine part of their own schedules and make choices about their lives added substantial risk and inefficiency to school operations. It threatened the very order of the institution's custodial model. Some students would make stupid mistakes. A few might even get into serious trouble. We could only hope they would make their mistakes on our watch before the same mistakes might later cause them permanent harm.

We started with two modest pilot programs to test an independent-living concept. Eventually all seniors would live in an apartment with three roommates each in a dorm-like building where two adults lived on the first floor. Each senior was issued a debit card and was responsible for buying his or her own groceries at local markets, preparing meals, keeping the apartment tidy, doing laundry, and carrying out all the other responsibilities of adulthood. Most important, they had to make daily decisions about managing their time and behavior. This was a real-life learning experience in adulthood, but one with a safety net. Our students were still obliged to follow school rules, go to classes, and obey the school clothing, grooming, and visiting policies. But now they had to rely on themselves.

It took more courage than smarts to introduce the first independent-living program for our older students. It was long overdue, and I was proud to participate in one of the most profound program changes ever made in the quest for student success. Finally, it felt as though Milton Hershey School was moving into the twenty-first century while firmly rooted in her best traditions.

My six-month tenure as acting president passed in a blur. I had the time of my life and had never felt a purposeful drive this intense. It took some time, but with the help of the board and our strong new Leadership Team, we restructured the entire school, got rid of the multi-age housing, and returned to the elementary-, middle- and high-school model. And we got the right senior managers into the right slots. Most important, the school had restored our founder's mission. We were once again serving the neediest and most vulnerable children we could find.

Meanwhile, the board continued its search for a permanent president. I figured I would either be "toast or toasted" seven months into the temporary job. I had not hesitated to make essential changes regardless of the consequences. As it should, the board insisted upon an exceedingly thorough search process that included many rounds of interviews, forums, and focus groups between the three finalists and the school community. The search committee included a houseparent, a teacher, an administrator, and an alumnus. I was delighted that the "school family" was so well represented in the process.

Yet I was really too busy to obsess about the search process. By June, it was time for the Class of '03 to go over the wall. The future of these precious kids took precedence over everything. Just days before commencement, my staff kidded me for "panicking" like a worried parent, as I repeatedly asked if there wasn't one more thing we could do to get our students ready to embrace their futures.

The staff reassured me that we had done everything we could and the kids were as ready as they would ever be. But I fretted and then came up with a last-minute idea. I hastily convened a luncheon where chosen staff members, each a Milton Hershey School alumnus, hosted a small table of seniors. Their assignment was to have a "no BS" discussion about the harsh realities of transitioning from the Home successfully. I made sure the food would be good, but it turned out the seniors were more starved for real over-the-wall stories. Even the most oblivious senior realized that the Milton Hershey School Meal Bus would stop coming in a few days. Some of them were feeling that cold welling up of panic at the imminence of their departure. Most of them were open to the coaching, and eager for tips; they drank in the cautionary tales of the graduates who had faced this same trauma years earlier. The luncheon has become an annual commencement-week tradition.

I called the Class of 2003 the "Class of Destiny." The name was a bit grand, but the kids came to like it and it reflected my passionate commitment to their success. I composed a rap ditty for them. I did the same for each of my graduating classes. The students got a huge kick out of my goofiness. Graduating senior John Monteban delivered the farewell address for his classmates. He paused at the end and looked directly at me and said, "Mr. O'Brien, no matter what . . . you will always be our president." His words meant a great deal to me and I suspect that the board of managers, which rarely heard the voices of students, heard his words that day too.

10

THE POLITICS OF RIGHTING THE SHIP

Getting rerooted in our Founder's ways. *Courtesy of the Milton Hershey School*

The official search for a permanent president was an intensive process that lasted for seven months and reportedly cost several hundred thousand dollars. Three finalists went before at least ten focus groups of houseparents, teachers, students, and alumni. As in any sound search for the head of a school, each of these vital Milton Hershey School constituencies had representation on the Search Committee.

A problem arose when the search consultant called to say he was unable to find a record of my master's degree at Johns Hopkins. He sounded excited. I was mystified. It was an indisputable fact that I had matriculated there and earned my degree. Upon further investigation, I learned that the university had lost my records when they switched from a paper to an electronic retrieval system, a pretty serious short-coming for a major university these days when confirmation of academic credentials is essential to career success. After asking a Hopkins professor and classmate to vouch for me, I went on a lengthy search of my own home and dug out my official diploma, tucked away in the attic. It felt weird to be relieved by this confirmation that a well-known event in my life had actually taken place.

The other two candidates for the job were from exclusive schools that served predominantly youngsters from high-income, upperclass families. These educators were talented and well qualified. Yet I was somewhat puzzled that the headhunter and the board thought their experience with affluent students was suited to our school and our students who came from far grittier backgrounds.

When the board offered me the permanent position in July, I was flat-out thrilled. And honored beyond belief. I had stayed immersed in the challenge and had loved every moment. Now I could refocus and redouble efforts to take on this herculean challenge. On July 30, 2003, I wrote in my journal, "My need: to stay grounded and humble in full service mode . . . savoring every moment by being present." I was coaching myself to continue to learn and improve and be in the moment. I felt so grateful for the privilege of being able to continue as a steward for Milton Hershey School.

The next day I wrote a letter to the school community about the honor of leading my childhood home. I wrote,

> In many ways, it feels like I have been preparing my entire life to pay back Mr. and Mrs. Hershey's life-saving gift to me. I know it is what I am on earth to do right now . . . it is clear to me that we have the chance of a lifetime to make Milton and Kitty's dream of saving and transforming young lives come true even beyond their rich imagination. Milton Hershey School will become this extraordinary place as

we get re-rooted in our Deed and history; value and engage every member of our School community; and pull together to prepare our precious children to become productive citizens. Getting MHS to be this exceptional "fountain of character development" is a daunting but very doable challenge.

The mountain was high, but I felt confident we could scale it because we had the mission, the dedicated staff, the devoted alumni corps, and ample resources. I was fortunate to have an exceptional assistant, Kathy Forney, who joined me at 5:45 a.m. every morning to kick-start the ascent. But first, we needed to shift the entire school structure to focus like a laser on child development. We simply could not tolerate a structure that prioritized order, efficiency, and staff convenience. The students had to become priority one. Period.

Many corporations become similarly hidebound and calcified by doing things the same way long beyond the time for change. No matter how difficult it is to change a culture, change is often necessary for survival. Too many once-successful nations, corporations, and institutions have fractured from within because of a refusal to change. Peter M. Senge, the director of the Center for Organizational Learning at MIT Sloan School of Management, famously wrote, "People don't resist change. People resist being changed."

I learned a great deal about resistance to change during my fifteen years as a change consultant for AT&T after the stunning divestiture decision handed down by Judge Harold Green in 1982. AT&T and its regional Baby Bells had held a monopoly on telephone service almost since Alexander Graham Bell invented the telephone. The government felt the monopoly stifled innovation and hurt consumers and ordered the huge conglomerate to be broken up into medium-sized parts. AT&T became a classic case-study in corporate transformation as it went from a quasi-governmental behemoth whose rates were set to guarantee predetermined profits to just another competitor in a Wild West marketplace with smaller, feisty telephone providers, including former Bell family members.

Suddenly, AT&T managers had to become leaders and customer-relations personnel had to become hardcore salesmen. The safest Fortune 500 company in history had to start to take great risks. Gus Blanchard, a Princeton classmate of mine, led the culture-change effort at AT&T by his own example. He designed an entire "curriculum" on change leadership and resilience and led all his managers through it. He asked me and Renaissance Leadership to lead the coaching effort, but he also changed the everyday work culture to reward risk, innovation, and transparency.

I focused on helping the corporate officers to get comfortable with large-scale change and risk-taking, then to embrace it, and finally to lead the enormous changes that had to be made. Even though the intellectual desire to change was clearly present, the comfort of decades of habit, routine, and certainty conspired to prevent vitally important visceral shifts in attitude and approach. Thousands of middle-level managers who had acquired inordinate power in the corporate bureaucracy resisted any change that threatened their traditional turf or control. Making matters worse was the unintended consequence of the downsizing. Lucrative severance packages were offered to thousands of voluntary "retirees," and many of the most talented and resilient managers pocketed the cash and struck out for pioneering positions with new, more nimble competitors.

We knew that transformational change required dramatic intervention. So we utilized experiential challenges such as outdoor rope courses, mountain climbing, and sailing adventures to reach our clients at a deep and visceral level. Faced with such daunting roles and settings in our outdoor workshops, the highly talented senior managers tended to revert to safe strategies. This led to failure and frustration, but eventually it also led to a willingness to reflect, learn, and risk new approaches. We videotaped their struggles and breakthroughs so they could witness their repeated failures and adaptive strategies. This was critical in getting past the ego resistance to change. We also introduced a circular feedback system that today is called "360 Degree Feedback" in which each leader gets candid direct reports on their efforts to become an innovative leader from their boss and peers. High-resolution "mirrors" are essential to personal transformation of this magnitude.

Our own cultural transformation at Milton Hershey School was not unlike that of AT&T. We needed to establish deep trust even while parting with senior managers from the old regime who clearly did not want to align with the new vision. Without trust, we could not hope to get our shell-shocked staff to shed their attachment to turf, comfortable routine, or limiting beliefs about improvement possibilities. It is human nature to struggle fiercely to maintain the status quo. The status quo validates who we are and what we have achieved. And more than anything else in my experience, people are obsessed with being "right" about their perceptions of themselves and the world around them. It creates the proverbial self-fulfilling prophecy. The most righteous people are even willing to be "dead right."

We elevated the vision of what was possible at Milton Hershey School given our noble mission and our remarkable access to phenomenal resources. And we rewarded transparency, selfless service, and well-intended risk-taking made in the cause of successful student development. In order to reach a fraction of our enormous potential, we at Milton Hershey School had to pivot and focus relentlessly on the success of our students and recent graduates.

The biggest hurdle I faced was getting our staff and students to believe the overall vision was achievable in five years. Very capable leaders would point to all the significant challenges to just getting the school stable and healthy again. Then there was the recurring question: "How do you expect to fix all these problems and grow the school to serve 60 percent more children while expanding to a year-round program?"

"Here we go again—another wild-eyed visionary," the murmurs began. One faculty leader, whom I respected, said, "Are you nuts? We can't do all this at the same time!"

"Yes," I answered. "Nuts like Mr. Hershey when he started building the world's largest candy company right over there in the middle of nothing but cornfields. While he simultaneously built an enormous workforce and their homes and an entire community for them and the trolley lines to bring employees from adjoining towns. All that while he was inventing a manufacturing process for milk chocolate on a large-enough scale to make it affordable to all." Since I was getting carried away, I added, "At least the cows didn't need to come home. They were already here!"

Heads nodded and bellies laughed in a way that showed me that folks were buying in. While they still thought I was crazy, they knew I was hell-bent on getting us up that mountain one way or another. More importantly, they all knew that far greater miracles had already been produced on this same soil.

The opportunity to turn my childhood home into a more nurturing place was something I could never have imagined possible as a child. As

HomeGuys, our expectations and hopes were limited by our experiences, which were circumscribed by the tiny world of our school. Those high walls that limited our vision were simply too great at that time for anyone to see over. My brother Frankie would have been utterly stunned to have seen me chosen to lead Milton Hershey School. I tried to imagine what he would have felt about this amazing honor, but it fell beyond the comprehension of the O'Brien brothers.

I had long since relinquished the illusion that Frankie's mental collapse came about solely because of bullying at Milton Hershey School. Certainly, the abuse was a contributing factor and caused him considerable pain. But I eventually came to terms with the history of mental illness in our father's family, a history that likely included Frankie. The fact that Frankie had witnessed our mother's murder at age four may have contributed to his mental collapse along with the serious car accident that caused his traumatic head injury. A perfect storm of devastating conditions hit my poor brother. Yet I would never say he did not have a chance. Every child has a chance, despite overwhelming odds. Milton Hershey School at its best vastly improved the odds. It only takes one moment, one caring adult, one slight shift in the cosmos to change the course of a lifetime. But my brother never got the breaks that might have helped him survive.

As an adult, I realized and accepted that I had little control over most of the factors that led to my brother's fate—most but not all. I could deal with one of the issues: the type of abuse and benign neglect he experienced at our Home. My tenure at Milton Hershey School became a crusade to make our school a kinder, gentler place for the children I called "the invisible middle." These kids were not high-profile athletes or scholars or demanding mischief makers; they were average kids. Children at the extremes, both the high-achieving, talented children at the top as well as the devilish ones at the bottom, tend to attract all the attention of adults at a school. The kids in the middle, the anonymous middle, muddle through as best they can.

To achieve our goals, role clarity and commitment were essential. The students needed to work hard, appreciate their remarkable opportunity, and strive to embody Milton Hershey School values. The staff and teachers needed to view their work as more than just a job. They needed to embrace their role as substitute parents of children who came from severe adversity. As our deep commitment to serve the neediest of children was realized, incoming students were now poorer, more troubled, and even less prepared for the academic and lifestyle changes at Milton Hershey School. These kids could try the patience of a saint at times. But every child deserved a chance. That is what we would provide, a real chance for every last one of them, the chance Frankie never got.

I admit I used every trick from my trade as a leadership consultant to make changes. I introduced a mantra, "Simplify, Stabilize, and Serve (Our Kids Directly)," to guide us through our first year. I helped re-write the school pledge to speak directly to the hearts of our kids and staff. Beyond the Spartan Peace Prize, named after Frankie, we introduced awards for random acts of kindness. I am convinced that symbolism matters and that visible acknowledgment and reward for good behavior reinforces the core message.

My staff rolled their eyes more than once at my constant cheerleading and hard-charging style. My insistence upon student outcomes collided sometimes with labor-union work rules. It was difficult to reconcile my respect for the right of each worker to have a union represent him or her and my intense demands that our children's needs take precedence over everything else. Most of the staff came to share my enthusiasm for a child-focused Milton Hershey School.

It was a terrible blow when my classmate and "brother" Dick "Percy" Purcell died unexpectedly in 2004. He was my best friend and mentor on this vital mission. After their mother had died, Percy enrolled at the school at the age of seven with his brother Milton who was four and who had been named for our founder. Their sister went to a Catholic orphanage. Percy and I played football, basketball, and baseball together and became inseparable pals for life. While I went off to college, he stayed in Hershey and founded a successful machine company that manufactured precision parts and machines for manufacturing plants, including the chocolate factory. Dick and his wife, Sally, spent countless hours as volunteers at the school and mentored dozens of kids. I created the Unsung Graduate Award and presented it to Dick posthumously the year after he died. A couple of years later, we named the Alumni Friendship Hall and Garden after him, a permanent memorial to a phenomenal HomeGuy who embodied the very best of Milton Hershey School.

I was deadly serious about restoring the school's mission. We began to enroll the children with the greatest financial, social, and environmental deprivation. The poorest and neediest children and their families were highly unlikely to find us. They were not middle-class families doing research on the Internet on a home computer. So we needed to find them through an aggressive recruitment program. We set up a group called Spartan Ambassadors in the spring of 2004 and charged this group of graduates with the task of helping our Admissions Office identify potential students for the school. We also formed strong recruiting partnerships with Head Start agencies, public-school counselors, and ministers across the Mid-Atlantic region.

We viewed each enrolled child, regardless of academic or social deficits, as gifted. Treating each kid as special would become a self-fulfilling prophecy. The children responded to the manner in which we treated them. A relentless focus on character and leadership development, personal accountability, and service to others made self-sufficiency, a work ethic, and self-discipline hallmarks of the Milton Hershey School experience but also led to higher performance and achievement by the students. It ought to be obvious that students who work hard, display enough discipline to do their chores and homework, and pay attention in class are going to be more successful than the kids who fool around and coast through school. The Milton Hershey work ethic was slowly returning.

The most frequent criticism lodged against Milton Hershey School was its failure to serve more children given its extraordinary endowment, an endowment in the range of our wealthiest universities, and the school's spending of spectacular amounts of money (ranging from $70,000 to $100,000 per child annually, depending upon how it was calculated) to yield rather regular results. Both are well-founded criticisms that come from smart, rational observers and should be part of the Milton Hershey School debate going forward.

On cost per student, it is helpful to hold up other expensive boarding schools for comparable illustration. Well-known prep schools like Phillips Andover and Exeter spend over $50,000 per year per student. If one assumes this as a rough basis, then what needs to be added to the Milton Hershey School cost model are over 100 more days of full service (Milton Hershey School operates 365 days a year), as well as all medical costs, clothing costs, psychological counseling costs, transportation costs, and food and shelter costs year-round. Add to that the cost of maintaining a ten-thousand-plus-acre campus, and, depending on which budget one is using, the cost of sending 90 percent of the school's graduates to college.

When you account for all those expenditures, the student costs appear more reasonable. But I agree with those who say it is still too high. We worked feverishly to reduce spending during my tenure, and we managed to lower cost per student practically every year. But it was tough sledding, and the savings were meager relative to the whole budget. So many of the major costs were fixed—including the largest item, staff salaries—due to union contracts and an expanding administration. The school could save significant monies by adding more children per student home and increasing class size, but those are believed to be the sacred strengths of the current Milton Hershey School model.

The real opportunity to lower cost per student is undeniably connected to serving more students. Most everyone agrees that the current year-round-home model begins to reach maximum scale as it approaches 2,000 students (there are 1,850 students currently). The Milton Hershey School Trust of $10 billion has sufficient resources to serve many more disadvantaged children, but the cost breakthrough only will come when a wholly new model is developed. Ironically, we developed several less-expensive but viable models with the board and a consultant during my last year at the helm, but none saw the light of day. I continue to enhance one of those alternative approaches on my desk today.

On cost, I will close with a quote I once heard: "It is easier and cheaper to build whole children than it is to fix broken adults." All that's needed to confirm that truth is our prison system and the costs (that exceed Milton Hershey School's costs) of our residential juvenile-detention system.

After "'03, the Class of Destiny," I created an identity and a little rap ditty for each senior class during my time as president. The ditties I rapped at school assemblies reduced the students to hysterical laughter. My staff howled as well. I did not mind acting a bit silly if it helped cement a strong sense of unity, cohesion, and school spirit. The tradition became wildly popular with seniors. At the start of each school year, seniors begged to know their class nickname. Among my favorites were "Knock 'em Alive '05," "Oh, Thank Heaven '07," and "Dare to Be Great '08."

Most of the staff joined in my obsession with graduate success, and our alumni became a powerful ally in this effort. Former HomeGuys and HomeGals, grateful for their own life-saving gift, came back over and over again to share their experiences with our students. These role models of success were a powerful incentive to our kids. Alumni recruited and mentored their "brothers" and "sisters" as the Spartan family came alive.

You would assume that the Alumni Association officers would be delighted that one of their own, a HomeGuy completely committed to the goals of the association, was now in charge of the school. We had returned Milton Hershey School to its mission to serve the neediest students and had begun the process of rapidly growing our enrollment—major goals of the Alumni Association. One of my first acts as president was to name four outstanding graduates to my Leadership Team. I wanted the alumni to be intimately involved in the school. We immediately convened meetings with the Milton Hershey Alumni Association and urged them to join the new administration as a partner. We offered them significant financial support and office space at the school. One proposal we made created space for the association inside Founder's Hall and made the executive director of the association an ex-officio member of our Senior Team.

While the alumni at large were overwhelmingly supportive, the association's leadership rejected each offer. I viewed the alumni as an important ally and actively sought their involvement and counsel. But our proposals were repeatedly dismissed. I finally came to believe that the Alumni Association, under its leader at that time, wanted to run the school itself and have full authority without any accountability. This is not its proper role. Alumni can advise, help, cheerlead, and contribute to the successful operation of a school, but no alumni association has operational responsibility.

It was inexplicable to me, and I finally concluded that it was driven by the contentious desire of one of the ringleaders to be in charge. He never supported the rebuilding process, and we finally had to give up on persuading him and his small band of supporters. Some battles cannot be won. We decided that the thousands of pages of personal and policy attacks he sent to the school and to the media and posted online were not worthy of acknowledgment. From then on, we never even mentioned his name.

The Alumni Association made a serious strategic error at that time. Instead of celebrating this "victory" of dedicated alumni leadership, they went back to court and demanded legal standing in all litigation involving the school. During the years when the alumni agitated for change and protested the deviation from Mr. Hershey's vision, this would have made some sense. Having legal standing would have strengthened our case for change. But once we had won the war, this battle was temporarily unwinnable. The association actually won the case in a lower court but was overruled on appeal in part because conditions had improved so much at the school that the association could no longer make a compelling case for change. This squandered an opportunity. The decision stands and can no longer be litigated. The ultimate "silver bullet" for legal standing for the alumni had been foolishly discharged.

Within a month of becoming president, I moved into a smaller office. I never liked the big old one. It seemed too corporate and conveyed a sense of majesty that seemed inappropriate at a school for needy children. In fact, we converted it into a large conference room, named it after the Bikles, and invited all staff and students to use it. I noted the move to the smaller office in my journal on October 14, 2003: "I like its scale and intimacy. It fits our children's home versus the grandiose one which was so intimidating and removed." I also made a note to myself that day to trust my instincts more and continue to directly engage with students every day.

I like to think that the appointment of an outside graduate provided some stability to the school after a decade of turmoil. The school family was somewhat traumatized from all the disruption and uncertainty of going off mission so badly. Having a graduate who was devoted to the deed of trust, even one determined to change the culture, provided continuity and hope that was badly needed at the time.

"Stability" didn't mean standing still. Our intent to expand enrollment required new facilities to house hundreds of new students. One of the early steps involved turning the now vacant Old Senior Hall, perched like a ghost on the hill overlooking the valley, into the main middle-school campus. To most Milton Hershey School alumni, Old Senior Hall is the "crown jewel" that physically embodies their Home.

It needed to be saved. Many educators believe middle-school is critical to childhood development. I have vivid memories of the challenges Frankie and I faced during those formative years, and I wanted to make certain our middle-school kids got the best. Middle-school children are old enough to begin making value judgments but young enough to be open to guidance and suggestion. Giving these kids their own first-rate campus provided them with a strong foundation for their daunting high-school stretch.

The enormous administrative burden of increasing enrollment and the physical campus by 50 percent while simultaneously transforming the culture was fatiguing at times. Just as I did when I was milking cows, I got to work every day before 6 a.m. to get ahead of the onslaught. There I could count on seeing Kathy Forney, who rearranged her family's routine to help me lead us through the darkness. When feeling worn down, I sought a booster shot by visiting our precious students. If the administrative pressures felt particularly oppressive, I headed to the elementary school, which was once again called the Fanny B. Hershey Memorial School after Milton's mother.

My favorite place was Mrs. Cook's kindergarten class. Christine Brennan Cook in 1981 was the first of nine females to receive Milton Hershey School diplomas. Chris and her classmates were true pioneers. She returned to Milton Hershey School after college as a member of the staff and has taught kindergarten for decades. She welcomed my visits. Visiting Chris's class always felt more like two "Milts" reconnecting than a boss checking up on a teacher. Her classroom was a place of warmth, stimulation, order, and love. It reminded me of my own kindergarten days.

Some of our new four and five year olds were shy at first meeting but would become "knee-huggers" within minutes. Chris would ask them who they thought I was. Invariably one would say, "Mr. Hershey." When she told them that Mr. O'Brien was president of the school, they were utterly unimpressed. I always loved that. When these tiny children crawled upon my lap as I read to them from Dr. Seuss or my favorite, *The Little Engine That Could*, I became acutely aware of their vulnerability. Small children are just so delicate, fresh, and innocent. Their entire lives lay ahead of them, and they are open to everything, both good and bad. As these little ones snuggled into my lap, I reflected on the recent trauma they had experienced by being uprooted from what they knew as family and dropped off at this big, scary place. But the secure climate created by Mrs. Cook allowed them to play, smile, hug, tease, and just be children with all the joy that ought to entail. This fragile trust masked a deep trauma that would take years of nurture and customized counseling for each of them to overcome. I felt grateful knowing they would get just that from our dedicated staff.

I often told Chris she had the most important job in the world. I meant it and I felt it. She reminded me of my favorite houseparents, Mom and Pop Arbogast, and the teachers and coaches who comforted me, taught me, and gave me the tools to cope with my own trauma and loss. I hope I told the houseparents, teachers, and counselors of the monumental significance of their calling often enough. I appreciated acutely that they held a sacred trust because when the classroom or student-home door closed behind them, they held the lives of these children in their hands.

If I just needed a quick "reality check with a chuckle," I stopped by Coach Guyer's office. Bob Guyer was actually a Hershey High School graduate, but no one had more brown-and-gold coursing through their veins than Coach Guyer. His whole life's mission was to mold character in our "youngsters" or die trying—and to occasionally win a football game, which he did way more than occasionally.

Bob was intense and no-nonsense. He kept everything simple, including his football system and his advice to me. "Just get back to the fundamentals," he would coach me. When I described a thorny issue, he'd say, "You're making it way too complicated."

"Trust, respect, honesty—aren't they our core values?" he would ask. We chuckled. I left lighter and more enlightened when I walked out of Coach Bob's office.

Coach Guyer was also a hardhead. He never deviated from any of his practices, routines, or game plans even when staff, friends, and opposing coaches advised him to change. My favorite example was his "no play," where his offense lined up but never snapped the ball in an effort to draw the other team off-side. Most teams use this trick occasionally, but Bob liked to use it often when our team needed less than five yards for a first down. After twenty-five years of Bob's featuring the "no play," every coach and player in the region knew what was coming, so it rarely worked. But Bob Guyer believed in that play just as he believed that the most hardened youngster in our high school could be taught self-discipline and respect. He still works miracles with our kids.

Another way I stayed connected to our new arrivals was as a mentor, or "copilot," to third graders. The copilot program was an initiative created by our staff to help transition and retain more of our new students. We were enrolling as many as 450 needy new children each year. My first year as a copilot, I mentored four freshly enrolled boys. I only spent an hour every week with them, but I was completely exhausted by the end of each sixty minutes. Their disinterest, distraction, and misdirected energy drained every ounce of the patience I possessed and gave me a greater appreciation for the daily challenges faced by our dedicated staff. By the second year, I literally begged for girls to copilot in hopes they would be more receptive and engaged in learning. They were. The maturation of girls and boys occurs at a different pace. I have stayed in touch with many of those girls and cannot wait to hug each one on graduation day in 2016. I also focused on seniors. In their sports, music, theater, student homes and classrooms, and even assemblies, I exhorted them to lead. Something about the imminence of their going over the wall touched me. I challenged and loved them with equal intensity.

My relationship with the board began well. For the first few years, the board maintained an arms-length relationship with the school administration. They had hired me to rescue the school, and they supported our vision and strategic plan for the turnaround. I kept them informed of school operations and they let me run the school. It was not my job to engage in board activities, and I was only faintly aware of quiet changes taking place in the board's internal operations. I was the first Milton Hershey School president not granted board membership. Earlier, three presidents had actually served as chairman. The board's structure and governance lay beyond my influence or responsibility.

As I've noted, there was an insidious problem that lay in the original structure of the board: a lack of accountability and a self-perpetuating mechanism that encouraged insularity. In the summer of 2002, that historic agreement between the attorney general and the board, which I helped to negotiate, ended the practice of trust board members serving on other boards in the Hershey empire. To many alumni and the attorney general, multiple board memberships held by the same people created conflicts of interest. We wanted the board members to focus exclusively on the wellbeing of our students and our school. Shockingly, this crucial reform was rescinded within a year.

The board was made up of caring, decent people. I certainly had strong opinions about some of the decisions they made, but people can disagree. What is clear to me and only becomes clearer over time is that money in the astonishing quantities generated by the Hershey companies can be a corrupting influence. Money need not be inherently corrupting, but billions of dollars is just so much money that it distorts perception and behavior. Most people cannot really understand that kind of wealth. It is simply beyond our imagination.

In addition, the relative isolation and lack of transparency that most charitable boards, and indeed, most corporate boards, enjoy also creates a false sense of reality. In this posh, affluent environment, the normal rules and strictures simply do not apply. Board members can justify their behavior and actions to one another because they really do not answer to anyone else. They act within an echo chamber. They can make bad decisions and rarely pay the consequences because there is so much money that a bad investment or the expenditure of a few million here or there has little adverse effect on the bottom line. They also tend to select people who act and think just like them to join the board, and in this way they perpetuate a way of thinking and behaving that seems to them to be correct.

At this time, compensation levels at the highest levels of corporate America were skyrocketing, but it is my belief that charitable board members ought to be guided by a higher motivation than money. For example, I was deeply honored to serve on the board of trustees of Princeton University, my alma mater. Many of my fellow trustees were enormously talented people who headed up wildly successful enterprises. They would routinely donate multimillion-dollar gifts to the university. I never had that kind of money, but each of us was expected to make a "stretch" contribution to the university and none of us received any pay for serving on the board. We contributed money to our school. We did not receive any. This is as it should be.

To be completely transparent, I must acknowledge that Milton Hershey School compensates its employees quite well, starting with the president. In my contract agreement with the board, I accepted a salary offer slightly below that of my predecessor. Simple but lovely on-campus housing along with a performance incentive arrangement were also part of the package. At the board's insistence, all my retirement benefits were distributed in lump-sum payments each year of my tenure. I received no pension. When these benefits were combined, they sometimes exceeded my salary. My salary was less than I made at Renaissance Leadership, but it was substantial compensation in the education field.

By every measure examined by the board's compensation consultants—such as size of endowment, enrollment, and operating budget— the compensation of the Milton Hershey School president ranked near the middle of the pack of comparable institutions. It was lower than similar-sized colleges and about the same for smaller, exclusive boarding schools. Yet there was an enormous difference in responsibility. Milton Hershey School did not just attend to educational needs, and we did not shut down in the summer or for holidays. Milton Hershey School is unique in being the "parents" providing for all our children's needs 365 days a year. That's why I believed that a terrific houseparent and a great teacher were worth every penny of the generous pay they earned.

In one of those supreme ironies that make real life more amazing than fiction, the new "reform" board quickly became politicized. I guess it's not surprising that Harrisburg insiders made certain that friends and political allies ended up on the board. One of the most important "reform" board members was LeRoy S. Zimmerman, a prominent Harrisburg lawyer who had served as attorney general for two terms in the 1980s.

Sometime in the spring of 2003, the Milton Hershey School Board convinced Attorney General Fisher to delete all the conflict restrictions from the 2002 agreement. I was shocked. The most important and hard-fought reform of the board in the history of the school had been trashed in just months. The Harrisburg newspaper, formerly owned by a new board member, printed a story that seemed surreal to me. It said that elimination of the conflict provisions actually *strengthened* conflict-of-interest rules for the school's employees. This was an Alice-in-Wonderland-like up-is-down interpretation. It made no real sense. There had never been any history of problems with school employees and conflicts. It had always been powerful and affluent board members who had conflicts, and the board had been the target of those provisions in the 2002 agreement.

I will concede that appointing the same members to different boards may have made some sense back in Mr. Hershey's time: it was his trust and his money. But the sheer size and wealth of the Hershey corporations had never been envisioned by the founder. Nor could he have guessed how a self-perpetuating, all-powerful board might manage his $10 billion trust many generations later.

I was dimly aware of changes adopted by the board, but the school and students were my primary focus. It took a fine investigative journalist, Bob Fernandez, to reveal what had been quietly taking place during those years. After I retired from my position, Fernandez with the *Philadelphia Inquirer*, the state's largest newspaper and a paper known for its investigative journalism, published a series of stories on the board and its compensation. In July 2010, the *Inquirer* reported that four prominent Pennsylvania Republicans were earning more than a combined $1 million a year as directors on three Hershey boards. Trustee fees escalated from around $35,000 to as much as $130,000 a year, as voted on by the board itself over the course of three years. Once that pesky restriction on multiple board memberships went away, members of the board of managers appointed themselves to other Hershey boards. Then total compensation mushroomed from $35,000 to over $300,000 for several members.

According to the *Inquirer* and Internal Revenue Service (IRS) Form 990 filings, Milton Hershey School Board members who voted themselves onto the boards of the Hershey Company and the Hershey Resorts and Entertainment Company began to reap enormous fees. The chairman, who received less than $50,000 per year at the start, quickly escalated to a total compensation level around $500,000. The current chairman, an alumnus, who is now several years past the original ten-year term limit, has taken several million dollars from Milton Hershey School entities according to the IRS Form 990.

The *Inquirer* articles hung out a lot of dirty laundry. The newspaper reported that board members worked an average of five hours per week. They stayed for free at lavishly renovated Hotel Hershey, wrapped up in their own personally monogrammed robes, and enjoyed free rounds of golf at Wren Dale Golf Club, which they had bought with school money. The purchase of the golf club rankled the alumni. The board paid $12 million for the club, more than twice its appraised value, and spent more than $4 million to build a nice new clubhouse.

The *Inquirer* highlighted the fact that the clubhouse was partly owned by one of the Hershey trustees. The board claimed they needed to buy the golf club, which was financially troubled, to create a buffer for the school. In fact, they made me a party to their decision by asking me to write a memo saying the club would create a buffer. I wrote that if the purchase of Wren Dale was a prudent financial investment for the school, then, yes, it would also provide a physical buffer for our new middle-school homes. Mr. Hershey must have been rolling over in his grave.

In the middle of my tenure, the board made a startling move to substantially alter the mission of the 100 percent–owned Hershey Entertainment and Resorts Company (HE&R). As with most for-profit companies, the first objective for HE&R had been profit—that translated into a dividend paid to the Milton Hershey School Trust. HE&R varied in its ability to show a profit, which is a story all its own, but it had managed to pay a reasonable dividend to the trust in recent years. Now the board had approved a new mission that put profits and dividends in second place. The new HE&R mission stated the first objective as largely doing the company's work in a way that was supportive and beneficial to the community and Milton Hershey School.

I must confess that I was pleased by this new direction when it was first introduced. HE&R is a sprawling enterprise that includes renowned Hersheypark, Hotel Hershey, and Hershey Gardens along with the Hershey Lodge, two golf clubs, the Giant Center (the arena where the American Hockey League Hershey Bears play), close to a dozen restaurants, and many other properties—even the Hershey Laundry and a zoo. Mr. Hershey created virtually all of these amenities under his umbrella, originally called the Hershey Estates, as a philanthropic subsidy to his beloved community. Many of them, like the park, gardens, and zoo, were free to the public in the founder's time.

I was pleased initially because I could envision a myriad of ways the Milton Hershey School student experience could be enhanced in partnership with HE&R. We had already created breakthrough collaborations with the Hershey Company on job internships and a new "Project Fellowship" whereby corporate departments "adopted" a student home and developed an aunt- or uncle-like relationship to those dozen kids. Our children loved their new chocolate-company mentors. HE&R had recently joined that program, but the still-untapped learning opportunities for our kids were gigantic. So we began to tap them. Jointly with leaders of the Hershey entities, we sculpted a vision whereby "the community would become a rich, highly experiential school" for our high-school students. The program offered our students job-shadowing, internships, job-application and interview counseling, and my favorite, a culinary arts program as a career offering for Milton Hershey School students with HE&R as our partner. It was wildly popular.

The Hershey Company had already become very supportive of our kids and mission. Now we were extremely grateful for HE&R's assistance with our precious kids. But while those good deeds were happening, a disturbing trend emerged. HE&R launched a massive spending campaign that included completely rebuilding the Hershey Country Club; buying the Wren Dale Golf Club at an inflated price and building a new clubhouse on it; completely restoring the Hershey Department Store to become HE&R's new headquarters; helping to build a first-class Hershey Museum; and pouring over $70 million into upgrades at Hotel Hershey. It was one thing to excuse HE&R from paying a dividend. It was quite another for the board to use the Milton Hershey School Trust to financially back this for-profit entity. In his deed, Mr. Hershey directed that every single dollar in the trust be used for the benefit of the school's children.

More than $100 million was a steep price to pay to get charitable help from Hershey entities whose terrific employees were willing to give that help to our kids unconditionally. The *Philadelphia Inquirer* reported on these developments and cited a court petition from former board member Bob Reese that said that the $70 million investment in Hotel Hershey was opposed by its own managers "because the investment would never pay back to justify it." The newspaper published a photo of beaming board members standing under a banner at the renovated Hotel Hershey that read "Zimm's Palace" in huge letters to honor their chairman, LeRoy Zimmerman. Alumni leaders said that photograph spoke more eloquently of an entitlement mentality than any words ever could.

This all took place at a time when the board had shelved our commitment to increase enrollment to two thousand students, ostensibly because of the bad economy and reduced trust revenues. As someone who grew up at the school at a time when frugality was part of the mindset, I actually welcomed a certain amount of austerity in 2008.

Deep financial discipline forces a reassessment of all programs and close examination of the priorities and basic values of an institution. But I began to harbor doubts as to whether the school's financial issues during 2008 were solely because of our building boom to accommodate six hundred more students. And maybe, as Mr. Hershey figured during the Great Depression, this was an inexpensive time to finish our growth plan.

During the 2008 academic year, certian clues caused me to wonder if the board would be transparent and inclusive in its search for the next Milton Hershey School president. This led to my decision to stay on campus until the end of the 2009 academic year. Mushrooming board compensation and potential conflicts of interest were disquieting, but the possibility of a secret process to select the school's next leader was deeply disturbing.

Although the board of managers went through the motions of a national search, it wound up choosing someone much closer to home, their own former board chairman, to serve as the new president of Milton Hershey School. Anthony Colistra, who graduated from Milton Hershey School in 1959, had an inside track. He joined the board of managers in 1997, and when the board members began to get appointments to other Hershey boards, he was appointed to the HE&R board and remained there after his tenure on the Milton Hershey School Board expired. He chaired the board of managers for the first three years of my time as president of the school. First and foremost, Colistra was known to alumni leaders as a loyal party-liner.

The board held all the cards. The relationship between board members and the attorney general's office had become extremely close. The Alumni Association believed that the Harrisburg newspaper, the one local paper with the staff to really cover the school, pulled its punches because its former owner served on the Milton Hershey School Board. Even if the reporters wanted to be objective, any inside information they were getting was all from the board's point of view. At that point, there were no whistle blowers.

After I retired from the school, the board of managers' activities generated more media headlines. Robert Reese made serious charges of misconduct against the board in 2011 after he was allegedly pushed out by the Hershey Trust Company where he served as a board member and the trust's president. He was a former top executive of the

Hershey Company and grandson of H. B. Reese, the founder of the Reese Candy Company and creator of Reese's Peanut Butter Cups. Hershey bought the Reese Company in the 1960s.

Reese claimed that one trustee hosted an expensive political fundraiser at High Point (Mr. Hershey's mansion) with all expenses charged to the trust. He also charged the board with "improperly comingling funds in Hershey Trust" which led to an SEC sanction. At that point, the trust had more than $7.5 billion in assets. Reese abruptly dropped his lawsuit against the board two months later, claiming health reasons.

The investigation that the attorney general's office launched at the end of 2010 once again became road kill on the campaign trail in Pennsylvania. Attorney General Tom Corbett ran successfully for governor in 2010 and no longer had responsibility for charitable trusts. The investigation seemed to peter out.

In November 2012, Kathleen Kane, the district attorney for Lackawanna County, which is the Scranton area, won the election for attorney general. Kane was renowned for high integrity, transparency, and a relentless insistence that justice be served even in the face of inordinate influence and power. Her Charitable Trust Division now oversaw the Milton Hershey Trust and had an opportunity to see that Milton Hershey's children came first.

However, in the summer of 2013, Attorney General Kane announced the settlement of the attorney general's three-year investigation into fiduciary wrongdoing by the Milton Hershey School Trust. Perhaps because of the inordinate hope invested in Judge Kane's track record of tough social justice and staying "above politics," the tame settlement was a huge disappointment and setback for the alumni body.

While it changed the way board members would be paid, it still permitted them to pay themselves more than $1,000 an hour for meetings and to continue paying themselves over $100,000 annually as school trust members. The settlement did reduce the number of other Hershey entity boards to which they could appoint themselves from two to one.

It is essential to recall that Mr. Hershey, the founder, said in his deed of trust that all moneys in the trust should be used for the care of the school's children. His deed specifically provides that the "Trustee shall receive as its full compensation for the duties required to be performed by it under this deed . . . not exceeding the sum of One Thousand Dollars." It also authorizes the payment of "reasonable expenses which the Managers shall incur in the performance of their duties." Until the early 1990s, this is exactly how the board worked. They received no personal compensation. And the short-lived attorney general reforms of 2002 got the board focused upon service again, if only for one year.

The settlement did nothing to address the issues of term limits, age limits, or how the members of the trust are selected. These are self-determined bylaws altered to favor the needs of existing members on an ongoing basis. A self-perpetuating board that votes to pay itself millions of dollars and to frequently extend its term limits will never reform itself. Milton Hershey School and her orphans will need more aggressive help from Attorney General Kane moving forward.

11

THE CIRCLE CLOSES

Going over the wall with class. *Courtesy of the Milton Hershey School*

When I accepted the interim president role in December of 2002, I had promised my wife Gail that it would only take about three years to get Milton Hershey School back on mission, with a healthy culture and rapidly growing enrollment. I based the estimate upon the typical time it took Renaissance Leadership to help turn around a corporate culture. Now more than six years later, I felt the school had grown healthy enough for me to turn over the reins. With quiet satisfaction, I could return to my wife and our retirement home on the Bay. I also did not want to prolong a tenure of enormous authority and replicate the damaging patterns of the past. So it was time for me to go and let someone else lead our Home into its next one hundred years with fresh eyes, new energy, and, hopefully, no baggage.

I confidentially informed the board of managers of my intent to retire a full year in advance in order to give them ample time to find a great successor. I felt strongly that Milton Hershey School deserved a distinctive and exceptional leader who could build on the foundation laid by our remarkable team. Milton Hershey School is a unique combination of a noble mission and gigantic resources, two extraordinary tools in the hands of an able steward. We should be able to attract some of the finest leaders in the educational world. The board chose to wait until November, four months later, to make the announcement public. In a letter to my staff written just before Thanksgiving, I said, "You know the adage that if you genuinely love someone or something, you love 'with open arms.' I have loved my 'Home' for over sixty years and always will. I care deeply enough about MHS to let her go." It was true.

I let the school community know of my retirement at a special assembly. That assembly was both a huge challenge and a relief. I treasured the transparency I shared with the Milton Hershey School family, so keeping this secret from my colleagues for four long months had been hard. I breathed easier when the secret became public. Part of me, the vulnerable HomeGuy, felt my departure might smack of abandonment. As Johnny O., I had been the CEO, the chief encouragement officer, for a long time in our students' lives. From the podium, I emphasized how healthy and strong our school had become and the importance of a new leader for the second Milton Hershey century. I told them that my ties to Milton Hershey School were truly umbilical and that I would always be part of the school community.

As a macho HomeGuy, I had spent much of my life hiding my feelings and burying emotions so deeply that it took me years to find them. But now, I cried openly when I spoke about our founder's vision, our life-saving mission, and the power of vulnerability itself. I have been told that age brings emotions closer to the surface, so maybe it was impossible to keep them from overflowing. I like to think that maturity also brings more balance between head and heart so there is less distance between the two. I do know that I felt wholly content when I expressed myself honestly. At the assembly, however, I kept the mood upbeat despite the ferocious pounding of my heart. I wanted the message that day to reassure our Spartan family.

Yet leaving my Home, the students, and the staff proved to be more difficult than I expected. I knew from my leadership coaching about the importance of fully completing a chapter that is closing. I had coached plenty of CEOs into retirement after a merger or long career. It is crucial to achieve a sense of finality in order to have peace of mind and heart. There is a cliché that closing one door leads to the opening of another door. Like many clichés, it is true, but you need to firmly shut that old door first in order to open yourself fully to the next great chapter of life.

To complete this mission, I needed to say goodbye to our wonderful staff and fully savor every moment of this final academic year. I brought that spirit to each month, each season, and each major event. I relished the excitement of the last Cocoa Bean football game; the majesty of the last Founder's Day; and the poignancy of the last Spartan Peace Prize assembly. As I walked through campus, I consciously committed to my mind and heart the scenes of Founder's Hall, Old Senior Hill, the Homestead, and Purcell Friendship Hall as the months passed from autumn through winter and to spring again. I concentrated on each one, hoping they would be indelibly etched on the celluloid of my brain. And I especially got close to the Class of '09 who I would join on graduation day.

Mr. Fisher, our German teacher and former president, had taught us *Die Zeit hast flugelt* [Time has flown], and time did appear to sprout wings during those last months at Milton Hershey School. The way in which time speeds up with age is disconcerting. I remember how the school year could drag on endlessly during the cold winters of my childhood. Now as an adult approaching retirement, time passed in the blink of an eye. Suddenly, Commencement Week for "Simply Divine Class of '09" was only two weeks away.

I sat down in my Founder's Hall office and reflected on my Spartan tenure in my journal. Our remarkable kids were about to receive their final report cards, so I decided to grade myself. Of all of our ambitious objectives, what had we achieved? What dreams were realized? Which were missed?

Most significantly, Milton Hershey School once again was a year-round home for the children with the greatest need. We had expanded enrollment by almost 50 percent from 1,250 to 1,850 precious kids. We had finally launched a successful program to prepare our young graduates for postgraduate life with an independent-living experience that was now a permanent part of Milton Hershey School. The school was also now tracking college success rates and identifying the causes of success or failure. By providing a helping hand to our graduates in those first risky years after leaving Hershey, we saw success rates begin to improve even as college expenses were halved. A significantly larger number of our graduates who were better suited to career and tech training after high school enrolled in community colleges and other vocational-training programs. Some kids enlisted in the military. Others went straight to work, but now they had mentors and a safety net. We and they were rewarded by greater success rates as graduates received the postgraduate education most appropriate for them.

We were now back on mission, deliberately enrolling students who were poorer, had fewer adults in their lives, had lower IQ scores, and lagged farther behind in grade level than the students we had enrolled in the past. They needed more nurturing, more individualized attention, and more creative approaches. I am proud to say that our staff gave them what they needed.

This restoration of the core mission and facilities was done with Mr. Hershey's eye for quality. We not only rebuilt Old Senior Hall into a fourth major school building for middle-school students, we also added more than fifty new student homes, a new health center, the Springboard Academy campus, a recreation center, an alumni campus, and the independent-living dorms for our seniors. To preserve Milton Hershey School history, we also built the School Heritage Center in the former student home Kinderhaus—the oldest building on campus. The combined cost was about $500 million. It was a lot of money, but the investment in the school's future and our students was worth every last cent. Moreover, the school could afford it. Its multibillion-dollar endowment exceeded those of Cornell, Dartmouth, and Johns Hopkins combined! By 2013, the endowment would reach a breathtaking $10 billion. The expenditures not only benefited current students, but the rebuilt campus and expansion were poised to serve Milton Hershey students for its entire second century.

I took particular pride in rekindling some of the fundamental values that were so dear to Milton Hershey himself. A work ethic and accountability, two qualities that are often lost in today's affluent society, were brought back with a strong chore program, a restitution program, and a system of discipline that was sensible, immediate, and applicable to the behavior. The days when a kid could be severely punished because a houseparent or teacher happened to be having a bad day were gone. When one of our kids screwed up, clear and consistent consequences followed. This went a long way toward teaching our young how to manage their behavior, how to work well with others, how to interact with society, and how to achieve their personal goals. The renowned Spartan character of the old days was coming back.

Because character development was essential to a Milt's success, I felt strongly that effort and conduct grades needed to be just as important as academic grades in earning credits toward a college scholarship and in measuring the performance of each student. Now students could be rewarded for making the Effort-Conduct Honor Roll. This elevated the status of those who were less gifted in academics or sports without taking anything away from our naturally talented students. It fostered maturity, self-worth, and self-discipline, three characteristics essential for our vulnerable kids if they were to succeed in life.

Reducing bullying and creating a culture that put a priority on respect for all meant a great deal to me personally because this would make the school a safer place for boys and girls like my brother. Bullying has gotten more attention in the media in recent years because of heartbreaking stories of youngsters committing suicide after being targeted for ridicule, teasing, and abuse. Cyberbullying using social media to target a vulnerable student was unheard of in my time, but the damage caused by low-tech bullying was precisely the same and just as painful. The only thing that changed was the delivery system. We worked daily to establish a mutual respect that started with self-respect in each student. Milton Hershey graduates are once again admired for the respect they show others in all settings.

Among the many motivational speakers we brought to Milton Hershey School to serve as role models for our students, a few stand out. Colin Powell, who insisted on spending time with our kids on campus and who stood directly on the auditorium floor in front of them instead of behind a podium, is one of them. He spun adventurous tales and asked our students questions until they were riveted upon his every word. Then to drive home his message against bullying, Mr. Powell told his "Bull Elephant Story."

As I recall it, he explained that the number of fatal attacks by African elephants on members of their own herd had increased enormously in the past decade, even while the herds themselves were declining rapidly, mostly at the hands of poachers. He pointed out that researchers had finally made a startling connection between this decline and the increase in fatal attacks. Most of the elephants slaughtered by poachers were bull elephants, prized for their huge ivory tusks, and it soon became clear that the bull elephants had traditionally prevented bullying in the herds. But now the bulls were gone. "Not surprisingly," Mr. Powell noted, "when bull elephants were reintroduced from neighboring countries, the bullying and killing fell dramatically. You upperclassmen must be these bull elephants, do you understand?"

I will always treasure the parting words Colin Powell half-whispered to me as we said farewell at his car. He leaned in closely and said, "You keep being the bull elephant that you are."

Our most challenging goal of creating a values-based performance culture for adults as well as students will go on forever, but we planted deep roots from the start. From year one we created the Milton Hershey School Sacred Values. They included not only Mutual Respect but also the principles of Integrity, Commitment to Mission, and Positive Spirit. When internalized, these values generate the pride, discipline, and accountability essential for institutional excellence.

Values tend to be fuzzy concepts until you put them into practice, show their importance, and reward them. Our values of integrity and mutual respect were immediately translated into a practice of leadership transparency. I attempted to let every member of the Milton Hershey School family know what was going on at the school, and I insisted on being open with the board on all matters. It is fairly easy for an administration to deliver positive "dog-and-pony shows" to an uninformed board to minimize criticism. And many do. Indeed, our lives were made more complicated by our being forthright, but high performance can only happen in a climate of integrity and trust. We worked at telling the whole story.

Another stunning example of a value shift was the transformation of behavior at assemblies. When I arrived on campus, all-school assemblies tended to be rowdy affairs marred by unruly and disruptive students (unless they were sleeping). After we insisted on mutual respect and commitment to the greater good in the first month, students found their assigned seats and at least pretended to pay attention during assemblies. They then soon joined in spirited recitations of the Milton Hershey School Pledge and the Pledge of Allegiance and sang the National Anthem with gusto. By the time we got to Milton Hershey's birthday and Veterans Day assemblies in November, you could hear a pencil drop in the packed auditorium of 2,400 Spartans. A respectful assembly planted a seed of respect in everyone.

We also had shortfalls in reaching our goals. The most obvious one was the stubborn student-attrition problem. It was still hovering around 10 percent, and with our mushrooming enrollment, that translated into losing as many as two hundred vulnerable children each year. We were beginning to learn more about the root causes of attrition—homesickness and weak parent/sponsor resolve—through our new Springboard Academy. But those insights and our other research findings were too fresh to help us systematically improve retention right away. As we began to graduate close to 200 seniors, losing 200 other students meant we had to find and enroll 400 new children each year just to stay even. And we were committed to growing our enrollment. That meant enrolling as many as 500 frightened newcomers a year. The attrition problem remains a problem to this day.

Another unresolved challenge is the temptation at a school with a sacred mission like Milton Hershey School to succumb to the "mediocrity trap." When you are literally saving children's lives, it is dangerously easy to rationalize that getting most of these kids to graduation and 40 percent of those graduates to finish college is a heroic achievement. Because it is. But as a school that has virtually unlimited freedom, inordinate resources, and access to the student year-round, Milton Hershey School should be stretching itself toward major improvement every day. To do so requires a willingness to change, risk, and fail well beyond the comfort zone of typical institutional leaders. Together, our Leadership Team risked new ideas and worked hard on innovative solutions.

I didn't have the same nervous jitters during Commencement Week for the Class of '09 that I had for my first graduation with the Class of '03. The '03 graduates were not unlike Carmen, Percy, and me four decades earlier when we went over the wall far more alone, vulnerable, and naive than our peers from public or boarding schools. Now our seniors were making their terrifying solo flight into adulthood with a year of independent living under their belts and tons of coaching on survival skills. And for the first time, Milton Hershey School was claiming ownership of its graduates' success and failure through the age of twenty-six. We did what any good parent would do. We provided tutoring, housing during summers and emergencies, visits, emergency financial help, and the support any caring parent of means would provide their child during that rocky transitional time between childhood and adulthood.

So I was more relaxed but just as totally psyched for the "Simply Divine Class of '09" commencement. We would be going over the wall together. But just as we were launching Commencement Week, a virulent strain of swine flu invaded our campus. Thank God we were accustomed to adversity. We could handle the flu. This highly infectious influenza, first detected in pigs, had leapt to human beings and spread throughout the world, putting the very old, the very young, and those who lived in communal settings at particular risk.

Our campus was no longer as isolated as it had been in my childhood. The World Health Organization raised the worldwide pandemic alert level for swine flu to its highest alert level that June. Dozens of our students and many staff members succumbed to fever, chills, muscle pains, diarrhea, and vomiting. It was a public-health nightmare, a huge administrative challenge, and a potential game changer for commencement when alumni and our graduates' family members traveled to Hershey to witness their children earn their diplomas.

There are established protocols for outbreaks of influenza at institutions. We followed those practices. We quarantined our sick students and kept sick staff off campus. Yet none of the state or federal authorities we consulted could tell us how serious this flu was or how long this strain would last. There was no way to plan. We fretted about commencement and the senior prom, and we debated what to do about the students who were still healthy. Should we send them home two weeks early and suspend school for the year? Or could we find a way to keep our kids on campus and also keep them healthy?

My inclination was to push ahead, keep school in session, and keep graduation on schedule through strategic use of our health center, the

160 student homes, and dozens of large facilities on our campus. There had to be ways to provide medical care and loving attention to our sick kids and keep the healthy kids from becoming infected. I was guided by my central belief that we were Home for all these children, and for all practical purposes, we were also their parents. What would good parents do when their kids got sick? Would they send them away? Of course not. And was it appropriate or even moral to send out to dozens of communities sick kids with a highly infectious influenza that could spread the contagion?

Despite my strong feelings, most members of our Leadership Team disagreed with me. They pointed out the complications of forcing teachers and houseparents to work in an environment that posed a risk to their health and the health of their own families. Our staff was already depleted by the infection, so could we orchestrate the housing, health care, and transportation of 1,800 students on a daily basis?

I deferred to the judgment of the team. They made a strong case, but more important, I trusted them and their collective judgment. In just a few months after I was gone, they would be held accountable, so it was only right to give their views heavier weight than my own. Our board of managers came to town for the commencement, and they agreed we should end the school year early and remove our children from campus. So the decision was made.

But I would not compromise on commencement. We shut down the school five days before graduation and sent everyone home except for the seniors. Most of the staff recognized the importance of commencement to the seniors, who had worked so hard for their diplomas. I could only imagine how a "lifer" would feel to be denied the chance to walk across the stage at Founder's Hall for a diploma after waiting and working so hard for fourteen years. From a practical standpoint, commencement would only be a miniature version of the typical celebration we held each year, but I was determined to give our Divine Class of '09 a classy sendoff.

The unions representing houseparents and teachers asked that their members be excused from attending commencement, citing health risks. We honored the request. While a small band of stalwarts would not miss the ceremony, it was sad to see more than half of the 2,800 seats in the auditorium empty. However, the parents, relatives, and sponsors of our graduates showed up in full force. Few had the financial means to stay overnight in a hotel, so many made long drives that began in the dark hours of early morning to get to the campus on time. Despite the challenges, they showed up, dressed in their Sunday best. For some in these very poor families, Sunday best was a clean pair of blue jeans and a baseball cap.

One beaming grandmother came up to me and whispered, "The swine flu be damned!" as she moved into the seat at the front of the hall usually reserved for Milton Hershey School staff during commencement. But in 2009, the graduates could see the smiling faces of proud mothers and grandmothers gathered before them as they marched across the stage. Most of the students and faculty still on campus watched the ceremony on closed-circuit television from a medically safe distance.

I was strongly advised to skip commencement and told that if I did attend, I needed to drop my habit of hugging graduates. I shook more hands and hugged more of my new "brothers" and "sisters" than ever. I also broke our tradition of bringing in a costly celebrity speaker to deliver the main address. I was going over the wall too with my 161 HomeGuys and HomeGals and wanted to have one more heart-to-heart talk with them. The graduates understood that this HomeGuy's journey was running parallel to theirs, and earlier in the day they had presented me with an official 2009 diploma, making me a member of their class. Could I get any more choked up?

I opened my remarks by declaring, "There ain't no swine can stop '09," to the cheers of the graduates and their families. I used the swine flu as a teaching moment and told them that this scaled-down commencement was just one more bit of adversity for a student body that had learned from a tender age how to overcome major obstacles in life. I quizzed our seniors on what our Milton Hershey School Sacred Values meant and how they translated into everyday life. To the delight of their families, the graduates nailed every one. I was so proud of them. The sacred values of Integrity, Mutual Respect, Commitment to Mission, and Positive Spirit had become part of each graduate. I used the address to remind our graduates of one more value, Mr. Hershey's unflinching generosity. I talked to them about the difference between givers and takers. As I did, I glanced at the board of managers who sat on the stage. I said, in effect,

> You have been given so much by Milton Hershey, the man, and Milton Hershey, the school, that you may feel like a taker right now. But remember, in order to pay it all back, Mr. Hershey did not ask that you be a doctor or astronaut or board member. All he asked is that you be a good citizen who gives back to his community.

As each of the newly minted graduates marched out of Founder's Hall, I knew three things for sure. One was that we had indeed given the Class of '09 and their parents and sponsors a classy commencement. While it was terribly sad to be without most of our sensational staff and student body, we had preserved everything sacred and uplifting about the graduation ceremony. I am confident that no "Divine '09" graduate will ever forget his or her unique commencement.

The second truth was that I was every bit as much a "taker" as any of these seniors. Milton Hershey School had not only saved my life as a child, it had given me the ultimate opportunity in life: a chance to serve a noble mission. In this case, that mission was to restore Milton Hershey's school and save the lives of thousands more needy children. I too would have to go forth and be a servant-citizen to repay this enormous gift.

The third truth was simply that I had given my all and my best to Milton Hershey School. The cause consumed me and my life for six thrilling years, and I could walk away spent in the advancement of this noble cause.

12

LESSONS LEARNED

"For the Shade it will bring to others"—Johnny and dear classmates. *Courtesy of the Milton Hershey School*

After launching our seniors on their wonderful but terrifying solo flights, I spent my final month as steward of Milton Hershey School focusing upon the lessons learned. My successor had been anointed; Milton Hershey School had begun its second century; and the swine flu had abated.

Some practices we adopted at the school were unique, tailored to our unusual student body and the challenges they faced. But our experience at this exceptional school also revealed universal truths that could have widespread applicability in education. While we had accomplished a great deal during those six and three quarters years, I believed that understanding why our initiatives worked or failed was critical for sustained improvement. We had to mine the "nuggets of wisdom" if they were to help others.

NUGGET NUMBER 1: ADVERSITY CAN BE A HUGE ADVANTAGE

All HomeGuys and HomeGals had experienced significant adversity in their young lives. From losing their parents and home to being abused and abandoned, each child had suffered trauma and sustained scars that would last forever. This adversity could be crippling. Or it could be empowering. We discovered the difference depended heavily on how we helped our children cope with "their story." In its first sixty years, Milton Hershey School tried to equip traumatized boys with a mighty work ethic, self-discipline, and an exterior toughness which could help them grind through the harsh realities of independent adulthood. And it worked for those of us who were favorably disposed to high achievement.

But because little attention was paid to interior and emotional health, many of our brothers lacked the emotional maturity or coping skills to thrive on their own. The contrast between Frankie's path and my own is a dramatic example, but there were hundreds of traumatized graduates in our era. When students overcame their adverse circumstances, it was a beautiful thing to see. We referred to this at Milton Hershey School as "getting the lights turned on" for our charges. Somehow they realized that they had triumphed over daunting challenges, that there was little to lose given where they had started from, and that they were well prepared to make something of themselves. Their adversity had been turned into a strength. It had become a significant advantage relative to advantaged kids whose character had not been forged by overcoming dramatic misfortune.

Perhaps our best motivational speaker ever at Milton Hershey School was Erik Weihenmeyer, who wrote *The Adversity Advantage*, a book based upon his amazing achievements—like climbing Mount Everest—even though he is blind. He implored our kids to take risks to climb out of their own "darkness."

NUGGET NUMBER 2: ADVERSITY MUST BE OWNED TO BE OVERCOME

While every Milton Hershey School kid has a sad "story," HomeGuys, prior to coeducation and the breakthroughs of modern psychology, honored the manly practice of suppressing their genuine tale of victimhood. It was considered weak and therefore dangerous to whine about one's misfortunes. And little adult help was available. There was only one part-time psychologist in my era, and it was highly risky to be seen near her office.

By the 1990s, the school had realized the importance of helping kids confront their victimhood by telling their stories in a way that allowed them to own their circumstances and take accountability for creating their "new story." It didn't always work because some students got stuck in their old tale and wallowed in the "feel good—woe is me" aspect of being a victim. So we pushed them to tell the accountable version. More and more Milts were able to move from being victims to owners of their destiny.

NUGGET NUMBER 3: KIDS NEED ADVOCATES TO BECOME ACCOUNTABLE

Few children have the capacity to make sense of abuse, abandonment, or even simple neglect. In order to navigate through mystifying trauma at a tender age and take ownership for your childhood tragedy, you need deeply caring adults. Lucky me—I had the Arbogasts, Coach Klingler, and teachers like Fisher, Hess, and the Bickles. They helped restore my dignity and worth from the inside out by having high expectations of and for me and believing I was special. If I take one sacred truth from Milton Hershey School, it is that even severely disadvantaged youth have a good chance of making it if they have at least one passionate advocate.

Milton Hershey School has come light years since that time when there was only one part-time psychologist on the staff. Today the school has at least forty professional staff in its Psychology and Social Services Division devoted to the emotional and spiritual health of our kids. And they support the hundreds of houseparents, teachers, and coaches who are passionate about helping our vulnerable youngsters make this transformational trip to accountability. Fully owning your life journey (being "i-count-able," I call it) is the most empowering and liberating mindset of all our attitudinal choices. For disadvantaged children, it is an essential bridge to be crossed.

NUGGET NUMBER 4: VULNERABILITY IS A STRENGTH

If we did know what the word "vulnerable" meant in high school, and I didn't, it would have scared our pants off. Just the thought of being open with our feelings, to admit we were frightened, or heaven forbid, to cry in public, seemed the equivalent of death. Everything about the old Milton Hershey School system was geared toward our being stoic, strong, and okay. What a massive charade. Over a thousand traumatized boys pretending we were okay.

You do not have to be a psychologist to know that you cannot fix a problem you pretend not to have. And our collective problem was lack of self-trust and confidence stemming from a repressed victim-story that we were clearly not wanted, not lovable, and not okay. Why else would our family send us away? To be vulnerable entails substantial risk that requires substantial trust. And the best way for Milton Hershey School students to gain self-trust is to confront their "abandonment story" head-on and take accountability for the future.

Today, Milton Hershey School has become very effective in facilitating a student's shift from victim to owning his or her life to—in the best cases—equipping kids to have enough self-trust to be vulnerable, to be authentic. One simply cannot be genuine without accepting and expressing authentic feelings and deeply held beliefs. Like teenagers everywhere, too many of our young Spartans erect false fronts and still cling to images of being tough, cool, macho, and untouchable. But with the enormous support and honest challenge of so many Spartan staff, the majority of today's graduates are acquiring a solid self-confidence based upon who they truly are.

It is fascinating to note that of the challenges our corporate executive clients at Renaissance Leadership faced, being willing to be vulnerable was chief among them. Certainly it is logical to expect that highly confident and successful captains of industry would exude self-trust and therefore express themselves freely. But when it came to needing help, harboring fear, or feeling lonely, many executives pretend everything is dandy. Much of that comes from the military "command and control" model of leadership that prevailed through the 1980s in corporate America: strong, stoic, and in control at all costs. And the cost is huge. If it is not okay to make or admit mistakes, then risk-taking is curtailed and both improvement and the learning curve suffer. If it is not acceptable to ask for help or to confess that "it's lonely at the top," then essential support does not materialize. When the leaders we coached became emotionally open and available to their people, performance and work fulfillment headed upward. Integrity works. And as Daniel Goleman has popularized in his books on "Emotional Intelligence," emotional integrity is the ultimate challenge for successful living.

When I returned to Milton Hershey School in 2002, one of the things I wished for was more longitudinal research on how our graduates were doing on important measures like career and marital success. With few exceptions, we had to rely on anecdotal information gathered at class reunions or homecomings. And while this information was not scientific, it was widely known that HomeGuys had an alarming divorce rate. Of the twenty classmates I stayed in close touch with, fifteen of us were divorced by the time we were forty years old. Lots of root causes were cited, but most of them centered on our inability to express our feelings. It was awfully difficult for me to apologize or even say I was wrong to my first wife. Expressing my anxiety about work or needing help—heck, needing a hug—violated my John Wayne facade. And I had no clue that there was a difference between sex and intimacy. Intimacy—warmth, coziness, family—was what I longed for, but my lack of self-trust made it terrifying. Most of us had gone over the wall without the gift and strength of vulnerability.

I have learned vitally important lessons about the balance of toughness and vulnerability while living on the Chesapeake Bay. Nature, I have noticed, is the ultimate teacher when I am smart enough to take notice.

The first lesson was delivered by a wonderful fish hawk called the osprey, which along with the bald eagle has made a remarkable comeback from the lethal use of DDT in the 1950s and 1960s. Every spring, the osprey return from Central or South America to the Chesapeake and to their same nest if they can. There they rebuild the nest, mostly on pilings or poles over the water, with sticks and branches, resulting in lots of jagged points on the inside of the nest. Since their very tender newborn chicks will be joining them soon, Mom and Dad pluck down from their breasts to make a comfortable nest-liner.

So far, just good parental instincts to make the home more comfortable, but here is where it gets fascinating. At the age of about three months old, the fledgling I'm told must leave the nest and make a solo flight either to land or back to the nest, otherwise it will die because a young osprey will drown if stranded in the water. This flight is bigger than going off to college or an adolescent's first day at work. Maybe it's analogous to seeing your kid off to war. It requires mega-motivation. What do Mom and Pop Osprey do to help? I am told that they pluck the comforting down from the jagged nest and make clinging to home an uncomfortable option! And the young osprey practice hovering over their nest before their daring first flight. That is precisely what our independent-living program is all about—getting our fledglings toughened up and motivated to fly.

The Chesapeake Bay's second revelation for me featured its famous—and scrumptious—blue crab. The adult blue crab has a thick, tortoise-like shell that is impervious to most any predator—well, except humans, who can and do kill almost everything that is edible in nature. But like all crustaceans, in order to grow the blue crab must shed its armor completely, and for a period of several days it is vulnerable to all kinds of predators! So these creatures are willing to risk their lives and shed their manufactured defenses in order to grow. Now obviously, these organisms do not exercise conscious choice to take those risks. What distinguishes us as human beings is that we are the only species that possesses the awesome power of conscious choice. So we can choose to use nature's enlightened role models to help us understand the strength in being vulnerable and the need to risk to grow.

It is interesting to note that the Milton Hershey School I attended helped HomeGuys be osprey-tough as we made our first solo flights. Then Milton Hershey School at the turn of the twenty-first century became nurturing and encouraged blue-crab vulnerability. What we worked hard to infuse in the Spartan experience during my tenure was the best combination of these virtues.

NUGGET NUMBER 5: NONTRADITIONAL STUDENTS NEED NONTRADITIONAL SUPPORT TO THRIVE

A shift from race-based affirmative action in college admissions to a broader effort to recruit all capable, socially and economically poor students is now underway. Many highly selective colleges have been widening their search for years. Since many high-achieving, low-income high-school seniors are not likely to apply to the nation's elite universities, those institutions must better understand the culture of these prospects in order to find and enroll them. For instance at Milton Hershey School, we found that creating strong networks with churches and school counselors and advertising free movie and pizza nights on TV and radio (most of our prospective families did not read newspapers) connected us effectively with our low-income candidates.

Providing an exceptional and inclusive experience for low-income students once enrolled is an even bigger topic on enlightened college campuses today. Most have found effective ways to help first-in-the-family college students navigate the culture shock they face upon arrival. Whether it is pre-freshmen summer programs, customized orientation, or thoughtful student and faculty mentor assignments, all help the nontraditional freshman with transition. Some efforts, like the highly innovative Posse Program, go much further. This national foundation forms multicultural teams of ten high-school classmates for the purpose of leadership development, prep for college, and then matriculation with many or all members of the "Posse" on the same campus. The special training and built-in peer support of the Posse in this shared, scary adventure is reportedly producing a phenomenal 90 percent graduation rate.

To serve first-time, low-income students well, colleges need to provide the networking, peer and adult support, and special counseling that these students have rarely had. What our deep experience and research at Milton Hershey School reveals is that low-socioeconomic students with limited family support are not only highly vulnerable during their college transition. They also tend to mask their vulnerability as much as possible in order to fit in and look fairly normal. So in addition to not being very good at asking for help, they are loath to do so. And like most undergraduates, they will gravitate to students who are like them, and these students will then collectively possess fewer of the survival skills necessary for their "foreign foray" into higher education. Some colleges like Princeton are championing the causes of diversity and inclusion with all-in commitments to bring the most promising low-income students to campus and to provide the optimum support to ensure they will get access to the exceptional Princeton experience. Well beyond passive acceptance of diversity, a big part of this initiative involves changing the culture to actively value differences in people, values, and practices.

NUGGET NUMBER 6: RESILIENCE AND PERSEVERANCE TRUMP INTELLECT

Hershey Industrial and Milton Hershey graduates through the 1980s were renowned for their grittiness. What we lacked in social grace, IQ scores, and sophistication was offset by a fierce determination to persevere through any challenge set before us. Prospective employers called it a "rare work ethic" as they lined up to hire our vocational students just prior to graduation. Milking cows twice a day, baling hay until the sun went down, and maintaining silence during "serious sit-ins" all contributed to our capacity to endure.

While perseverance is an essential trait for success for all disadvantaged children, it is insufficient if not combined with resilience. Working harder and harder has serious limits when not fused with "working smarter." Resilience is the critical ability to adapt to changing circumstances: to change direction, alter strategy, and even modify beliefs if necessary. Adaptive skills require practice at independent thinking and making critical choices on the fly. Until the 1990s, Milton Hershey School students lived in a static institutional setting that required minimal resilience.

To be sure, most low-socioeconomic children develop savvy and what some call "street smarts," but these tend to be coping skills that help kids survive rather than thrive. There is no greater gift we can give to disadvantaged students than a grounded confidence built by direct experience in their ability to adapt smartly to their chaotic world. That they become comfortable, even in their discomfort, is about managing change effectively.

Accountability, vulnerability, perseverance, and resilience are all vital attributes for success. Children in healthy homes with supportive parents have a decent chance of developing these virtues naturally. For impoverished youngsters, their only shot at attaining them is through deeply caring advocates at critical junctures along the way. All institutions serving vulnerable students need to find ways to facilitate more of these life-shaping and life-saving relationships.

Nuggets of wisdom materialize when you dream big, risk big, and look for the truth. Our relentless search for ways to better prepare our youngsters for success at Milton Hershey School meant we had to be open and transparent. Like the Chesapeake blue crab, that meant we were vulnerable to attacks by our detractors and critiques from our board. Occasionally we reverted to our protective shell with denials and reversion to the status quo. But not for long. Most members of our Leadership Team, and indeed most of our houseparents and teachers, believed in the nearly unlimited potential of Milton Hershey School to help our kids. While tempted, we would not rest on our laurels or succumb to the "soft bigotry of mediocre expectations." Intentional trial and error produced insight and progress. Those failures began to light our way to success. We dreamed big, risked big, and climbed a gigantic learning curve together.

With the sun setting on my immensely satisfying tenure at our Home, I documented the critical insights, opportunities, and threats for future Milton Hershey School managers. My life had truly gone full circle. My first conscious memories were formed at Hershey Industrial School when I was still a toddler without parents or a home. I found a new home, and like all orphans, I had many mixed feelings about it. This was no ordinary orphanage. There were aspects that were almost Dickensian, though we always had great heaps of healthy food, neat comfortable clothing, and a warm, lovely place to sleep. None of us had to plead for more gruel as Oliver Twist did in the fabled novel. The lingering negatives from my experience came more from being treated like a widget on an assembly line, and from the deep sense of abandonment I felt from losing my parents, my family home, and then my only known remaining family member.

One of the advantages of maturity is the opportunity to work through emotional issues over time. Eventually, I realized that my desperate search for approval and self-worth played out in an obsession with winning every accolade available at the orphanage. I had to be the best at everything to prove to myself that I was worth anything. So I captained most of the sports teams, won election as president of my class, became an all-state quarterback and salutatorian of my senior class, and won a full scholarship to an Ivy League college. Yet I often felt hollow and unfulfilled. External validation in a depersonalized institution could not mend my broken heart or save my brother Frankie's life.

I slowly learned that no amount of external recognition can do what genuine self-acceptance must do. I eventually worked through the feelings of loss that drove me so ferociously as a child and young man. My friends and coaches at Princeton helped me immeasurably. I came to terms with Frankie's decline and eventual death and worked through the guilt that haunted me. Of course, I knew intellectually that a young boy could have done nothing to save his older brother under those circumstances, but my heart forgave far more slowly.

I have been fortunate on my personal journey. I have had the opportunity to say thank you in a very concrete way to the institution that saved my life and to use the painful lessons from my boyhood and my brother's life to inform my leadership at Milton Hershey School. It may sound dramatic to say the school saved my life, but I am not the only graduate of Milton Hershey School who sees the role of the school in those terms. It is my deepest hope that the changes I helped to implement in the way Milton Hershey School operates today will help another troubled child and serve as a permanent memorial to my brother long after I am forgotten.

Life went on at Milton Hershey School without my involvement, except as an active alumnus. I elected to keep a low profile after I left. My relationship with the board of managers had deteriorated as I questioned the secrecy of the presidential search process in the final months of my stay. They hired one of their own to take my place. This was not what I envisioned when I gave them a year's notice about my intent to retire. The noble mission and inordinate wealth of Milton Hershey School enabled it to hire the finest leader in the educational world—preferably an alumnus with deep, visceral knowledge of this unique institution, but a leader with an empirical knowledge of poverty to be sure.

In the final months, a board leader encouraged me to consider an "emeritus-ambassador–like" position, but it felt too much like a muzzle and I declined. I would rather be independent and retain the ability to speak my truth. Then I was required to sign a nondisclosure agreement to get my final pension payments released. Almost all departing school managers were required to sign confidentiality agreements. I did. I have received no personal communication from the school or board since retiring and am rarely invited to participate in official events. When I go Home to visit favorite staff and students, I do so unofficially and in a low-key fashion. It's an exacting price, but one I am willing to pay.

Caution and insularity have been characteristic of the management of Milton Hershey's orphanage throughout its history. Sometimes adhering to tradition is a good thing. I certainly worked to reinstate the traditional values that governed the school because I believed then and believe today that those old-fashioned values of hard work, integrity, and self-discipline are just as important in the twenty-first century as they were in 1909 when Mr. Hershey signed the deed of trust. But excessive caution and resistance to change is at odds with the long-term survival of an institution.

The absence of true transparency and the absolute power of the board of managers continues to trouble me. It is the real fatal flaw of Milton Hershey's legacy. During that long year before I was named interim president of Milton Hershey School, the case for essential governance reform was laid out in stark detail. The state attorney general initiated these historic reforms, but the board lobbied successfully to rescind the most important changes less than a year later. This problem goes beyond Milton Hershey School. All charitable boards and all corporate boards could benefit from the same blast of sunshine, particularly in cases involving large sums of money. Trustees of virtually all schools contribute money. They don't collect it. Chief Justice Brandeis famously said, "Sunlight is the world's best disinfectant," and he is right.

Milton Hershey School has now been in existence for more than one hundred years and has harbored and educated tens of thousands of children. The "$10 Billion Orphanage" remains a little-known jewel nestled in the countryside of Pennsylvania. I wrote this book to let others know of Milton Hershey, the remarkable man and his legacy, and to highlight Milton Hershey School as a case study in what can go wrong and what can go very right in the education of poor children. There is no single best way to educate disadvantaged children. However, Milton Hershey School is one way that has a proven record of success in the lives of its graduates who continue to serve their communities, work hard in their chosen occupations, and raise their own families with the solid values Mr. Hershey espoused.

There is a cyclical quality to social sciences. There are times when institutionalization is viewed as a reform and innovation. Then decades later, it is considered retro and damaging. I have concluded that a black-and-white absolutist view simply cannot apply. I have seen too many children rescued from dysfunctional families and desperate poverty by Milton Hershey School to be anything but a fervent believer in the model. I have concluded that positive role models, an excellent education, and the camaraderie and care of loving caretakers can offset serious childhood trauma. All of these things give needy children the one shot they deserve to a full life of self-sufficiency and happiness.

I think about my brother Frankie every day. I remember him with a combination of sadness and fondness. The pain of his suffering and his difficult life will always be with me. But I know now that kids like Frankie who are blessed to fall into the orbit of Milton Hershey School today have the chance he never got.

Milton and Kitty Hershey had a dream for poor orphans. They would be amazed to see their school today just as they would be incredulous at the astonishing size of the trust fund and the remarkable advances in science, technology, and commerce that have taken place in the past century. Milton Hershey School is a remarkable school, perhaps the most remarkable school of its kind in the world. More than ever I believe in the potential of this institution to give poor girls and boys a real opportunity to heal from the emotional scars of neglect; to learn the skills and gain the wisdom every child needs to succeed in adulthood; and to thrive as strong, self-sufficient, and caring citizens. The only risk, and it is a considerable risk, is that the school's all-powerful overlords may neglect or misinterpret Milton Hershey's vision.

The saga of the world's richest orphanage will go on in perpetuity as required by its deed of trust. Significant good will continue to be done, and the serious challenges of governance reform and the need to serve many more children will remain. I will do everything possible to support my Home, but the journey has come full circle and is finally closed.

BIBLIOGRAPHY

Brechbill, Dr. Joseph A. *It Was Kitty's Idea* (2004).

Brenner, Joel Glenn. *The Emperors of Chocolate* (New York: Random House, 1999).

D'Antonio, Michael. *Hershey* (New York: Simon & Schuster, 2006).

Hobby, Rev. Dr. Clark E. *The Homeboy* (New Castle, IN: Clark E. Hobby, 1999).

Houts, Mary Davidoff, and Pamila Cassidy Whitenack. *Hershey* (Charleston, SC: Arcadia Publishing, 2000).

McMahon, James D. Jr. *Milton Hershey School* (Charleston, SC: Arcadia Publishing, 2007).

Milton Hershey School. *Milton Hershey School: Its Purpose, Goals, and Strategies* (1990).

Wallace, Dr. Paul A. *Milton Hershey* (manuscript, 1955).

ABOUT THE AUTHOR

Dropped off at the orphanage like soiled laundry at the age of three, **Johnny O'Brien** spent his entire childhood at Hershey Industrial School (later renamed Milton Hershey School). He credits the school with saving his life, but the rough-and-tumble orphanage of the 1950s put his older brother Frankie's life in peril.

Astonishingly, Johnny went on to be a fine scholar-athlete at Princeton while Frankie languished in a Pennsylvania state hospital asylum. The author would become a Princeton trustee in 2006, but not before being asked to play two fateful roles at the Hershey orphanage. The first was to help lead an alumni protest to save the soul of Milton Hershey School, which was being taken off its mission by a self-appointed board. When a decade of rebellion was successful, Johnny was then miraculously asked to restore the Milton Hershey mission as the school's eighth president . . . to save the school that saved his life.

Johnny's career featured education reform and leadership with twenty-five years devoted to being CEO and founder of Renaissance Leadership, where he worked with corporate executives to build exceptional teams through a culture of integrity and servant leadership. *Semisweet* is a natural extension of his mission.